TOWARD A CELESTIAL MARRIAGE

TOWARD A CELESTIAL MARRIAGE

DOUGLAS E. BRINLEY

Bookcraft
Salt Lake City, Utah

Library of Congress Catalog Card Number: 86-71295
ISBN 0-88494-602-9

5th Printing, 1993

Printed in the United States of America

To my sweetheart
Geri

Acknowledgments

The writing of this book could not have been accomplished without the influence and guidance of many people. I am grateful to Dr. Stephen J. Bahr and Dr. Wesley R. Burr of Brigham Young University, who encouraged me to pursue my study of family relations. I am also grateful to Sharon Berger, Marilyn Foutz, Eldon Haag, Jack Steele, and my father, Eldon D. Brinley, who were kind enough to read the manuscript and make many excellent suggestions. My special thanks go to George Bickerstaff of Bookcraft for the improvements his editorial skills have worked upon the manuscript.

I of course take sole responsibility for the material in the book.

To my wife, Geri, and my children—David, Terri, Becky, Jonathan, Andy, and Mandy—I express my deep love and devotion. They have taught me much about these sacred matters.

Contents

Introduction

As Latter-day Saints, our commitment to establish and foster strong, happy families is at the very heart and core of our theology, our lives, and our personal happiness. God has ordained family life as the means whereby his work moves forward (Moses 1:39; D&C 132:63), and we have the opportunity here on earth to experience, on a small scale at least, the heavenly pattern of marriage and parenting. The essence of our religion is that godhood and family life *may* be synonymous. We value marriage and family life as the way to learn and apply the gospel in our relationships with others in preparation for an eternal family experience.

Then, I think about my own experiences in teaching and working with families who struggle desperately for some measure of happiness—far below what God has outlined for us. Too many, it seems to me, are frustrated in marriage and rearing children—frustrated beyond what is a normal and important part of our own growth processes. Certainly family life is more complex and challenging now than at any time in history, and it calls for the very highest and best in us. But that is our task—our privilege really— and we must be equal to it. The Lord knows the scope of our challenge and our ability to respond. He has a great interest in our success since we are his children, and *our* children, after all, are *his* offspring, too. I am convinced that he has clearly revealed the keys to enable us to succeed and to strengthen our marriages and to rear righteous children.

Marital Stability

How well are we succeeding? When we look at the marriages of Church members in general, we see some cause for alarm. Sobering and disturbing statistics published earlier in the 1980s raised a concern over our "marital stability," the measure of whether couples stay together. The *Church News* reported figures from a cross-sectional survey of marrieds which showed that one-third of our membership (32 percent of men, 35 percent of women) experience a divorce by age sixty! (See *Church News*, 6 Nov. 1983, p. 4.) Although this survey was a random look at Church membership rather than a study on temple marriages, these figures were shocking to me.[1] We have always known that temple marriages are very resistant to divorce, but I had hoped that our emphasis on the permanence of marriage might carry over into all marriages.

But haven't we all been dismayed at the number of couples we know who are separating? Some of them *are* temple marriages. Have we not been jarred in learning that close friends, associates, neighbors, and sometimes members of our own extended family have separated or are in the process of seeking a divorce?

Marital Satisfaction

And what of those with intact marriages—those still together? What of the quality of their unions? Can we

---

1. This same report confirmed the stability of temple marriages. See *Ensign*, July 1984, pp. 78–80.

assume that if a couple remains married, their marital satisfaction is high? A study of United States marrieds two decades ago[2] suggested this breakdown:

20 percent had "ideal" marriages; each partner rated the marriage fulfilling and satisfying.

30 percent were "friendly and congenial," but well below the satisfaction level of the first group.

30 percent admitted that marriage began well for them, but schedules, work, other interests, distractions, and routine had taken their toll on the couple's happiness. They were now "de-vitalized," bearing signs of a "business arrangement" rather than a strong marriage.

20 percent were conflict-oriented—bickering, critical, negative, struggling; yet they remained married to each other.

Would this typology hold true today? Does it hold true for our members? Does it fit with your perceptions? Very little research has been done on the quality of Latter-day Saint marriages, and we do not have any current data on this subject.

Resolving Difficulties

In general, helping those with marital difficulties is not an easy task. Usually bishops or professional counselors are the last to be involved. Much of the damage to the relationship has already been done by the time they are called in. Hearts have hardened, defenses set. Let me share a typical experience. Normally it is the wife who calls for an appointment. (Very few husbands initiate "the call.") Nancy tells me on the phone that her husband is willing to come with her. (Many husbands won't come in with their wives.) As I greet Nancy and her husband, Bill,

---

2. Cuber, J. F., and P. B. Harroff, *The Significant Americans* (New York: Appleton-Century-Crofts, 1965).

they appear to me to be in their thirties and I learn they married in the temple some twelve years ago. They look to be an intelligent and attractive couple. "How can these two be so unhappy?" I mutter to myself. "They ought to be thrilled with life and deeply in love after that much time together." I learn that they have three children—two boys and a girl. Bill has a good job as a computer repairman, and they have their share of nice things.

It soon becomes obvious, however, that they are struggling with some very difficult problems. They are angry with each other, defensive, blaming one another for their estrangement, their predicament, and they want to quit if "things" do not change. There is no infidelity, no physical abuse, no third party tearing them apart. Yet they have concluded that a divorce is better than going on as they are; that their little innocent children will understand their reasoning, somehow, and survive a split without any serious emotional scars. They have come for one last try at reconciliation, or to confirm their decision to part. They hope I may have some "magic" to work on their partner!

This always seems to be such a tragedy. Divorce is never easy. I often think that if individuals knew what hardships divorce would bring and they worked as hard to repair their present relationship as they would struggle once they are separated, they could make it work now.

Since this pattern appears with some regularity, I find myself looking more closely at the dimensions of dating, courtship, marriage, and parenting. Perhaps we take this process too lightly. Maybe our young people grow up believing that all it takes to be happy in marriage is to be sealed to another member of the Church in the temple. Maybe we "fall in love with love" too easily (it doesn't take long on TV), and we become conditioned to think of marriage as the solution to loneliness and the beginning of a life of happiness.

Of course, helping couples like Bill and Nancy is a sobering challenge. This is sacred ground—make no mistake about it—intervening in the lives of struggling families, assisting couples to put their lives back in order, to reignite the flickering, dying, embers. It is a humbling experience. I find myself wondering how best to help them. I wonder what the Lord, or his prophet, would do or say were he in my place. Sometimes I will ask the couple: "Suppose you were telling all of this to the Lord rather than to me? What do you think he would say to you two?"

The answers vary according to the humility and mood of the couple. "I think he would be disappointed in us." "I think he would put his arms around us and tell us we need to start living the gospel again." "I think he would spank us and send us home and tell us to grow up!" "I really don't know what he would say." One responded, defensively, "If he were married to her, he'd feel the same way I do!"

"Do you think he would suggest that you divorce?" I query.

"No."

"Do you think he would discuss your communication skills?"

"No."

"Do you think he would tell you that you married the wrong person?"

"No."

"Do you think he would tell you who is right or wrong in this matter?"

"No."

"Neither do I."

I imagine that the Savior, or his prophet, would review eternal principles, principles that are, for the moment, lost or forgotten. I think he would remind each partner of the purpose for which marriage and family living was ordained, and of its place in the eternal plan of happiness. I think Jesus would share his atonement and explain its application to their lives. He would speak of covenants, of a softened heart, of forgiving one another, of repentance, of humility, of charity, of gaining his Spirit once again, of changing natures, and of breaking ingrained, negative habits. Perhaps he might even chastise. But, above all, he would teach, renew their perspective, and review the purpose for which this sacred relationship was instituted.

And almost always I ask, "Are you two praying together?"

"No."

"Have you ever prayed together about resolving these problems?"

"No."

"Have you ever prayed together?"

"Yes, when we were first married."

"Why did you stop?"

"I don't know. We just didn't feel like it anymore and got out of the habit."

"What are you doing together now to make things better, to enjoy each other, to renew your love?"

Not much, it turns out. *It is clear that the practice of human kindness and charity fades when spiritual resources are ignored, forgotten, and left untapped.* Once couples lose the Spirit of the Lord because of the way they treat each other, bad things happen in their relationship: sarcasm, anger, retaliation, criticism, defensiveness, power struggles, self-betrayal. All of these negatively affect marital happiness.

On the other hand, when the eternal perspective of marriage is clear and vibrant, we see ourselves as responsible stewards over a spouse and God's children. We are honored with the privilege to enter mortality, find an eternal companion, and savor the experience to walk hand in hand through a fallen world skillfully designed by Satan to trap us and thwart us in our eternal goals. We are eternal partners on an eternal team, passing through time and space on our own personal adventure toward exaltation. Our hearts are softened, our commitment genuine. We know we can't make it without each other. Our commitments carry us forward, the gospel giving us a sense of destiny and partnership with God. We must control and overcome the "natural man" and reach out to fulfill our callings as sons and daughters of heavenly parents.

Without such theological perspectives, however, secular exercises designed to improve our relationship and our communication skills (the common tools of counselors and marriage books) will never work any permanent change in one's heart: *they simply develop more clever and skilled fighters!* When a man's heart is right with God, his spouse, and his children, then improving his skills and his practice of human relations is rather simple. He will want to be better for the right reasons. He will understand that he has a mission to perform for the Lord. Alma taught that lesson long ago when he resigned as chief judge in order to preach the gospel and cry repentance in an attempt to soften the hardened hearts of his people (Alma 4:19). Our missionary system is based on this premise: Change first the inner man by teaching him of his identity as a child of God and of his purpose in life, and he will monitor his own behavior for the good of the social order. Only the gospel of Jesus Christ can make *lasting changes* for good in the hearts of men.

Therefore, we need two things: (1) true theological perspective that provides meaning and direction to our existence and destiny, and (2) lots of practice in applying the principles of the gospel in Christlike ways in our relationships with others. While that sequence is ideal, it can work both ways—as many converts to the Church have proven. Charity, however, is more easily implemented when its theological base is planted firmly in our hearts.

We live in a world pondering the fate of the family, sometimes casting it aside for shadowy imitations or desecrating its sacred and holy purposes. Alternative life-styles are espoused, for example, in blatant opposition to the plan of God. They are an affront to our Heavenly Father (Moses 7:32–36).

Of course, not all who marry succeed. Some divorces may be necessary to prevent physical, verbal, or mental abuse. Those who feel the need to divorce to protect children or preserve their own mental and physical health need our genuine love and acceptance. When an individual determines that divorce is the only sane option open, it is not our place to judge or withdraw the hand of fellowship. We are brothers and sisters and must assist each other through the difficulties associated with families in such times of crisis.

Marriage is a sacred trust. Those who trifle with covenants, or who destroy the spirit and love of a spouse or a child—especially if it is through transgression—will one day answer to a disappointed Lord. Jesus' words ring out, "Moses because of the hardness of your hearts suffered you to put away your wives: but from the beginning it was not so" (Matthew 19:8). Too often divorce stems from repeated transgressions on the part of one or both parties to the marriage. Worn down by abuse, bickering, and tension, one partner may select options counter to covenants and eternal happiness. The results are heartbreaking.

God has ordained marriage as the means of bringing his children to mortality. If as Latter-day Saints we fail in that assignment through our negligence or disobedience, his work suffers, and our salvation may be in jeopardy. It is our privilege to model for the world what God intended marriage and family life to be. It is a task of the highest priority. He needs righteous families to carry out his grand design. People of courage are wanted and needed to move this work ahead.

I seek to expand on these themes in the pages ahead.

Perspectives   I

The Family   1

The workshop from which all human beings emerge is the family. Each of us is the product of a family experience which might have ranged from a very healthy to a pathological environment. But it is at the family hearth that we gain much of our orientation toward right and wrong, and toward life in general. Consequently, the family is of immense sociological and, for Latter-day Saints, theological importance. Gospel teachings direct us to develop into healthy individuals who can attract a mate, consummate a marriage, and bear and rear healthy children. The pattern is then repeated by the next generation. The earth was created for this very purpose (D&C 49:15–17).

When families prosper, individual character is developed and refined, powerful family bonds are forged, and the Lord brings to pass "the immortality and eternal life of man" (Moses 1:39). When the family thrives, society increases in strength and vigor.

Most people marry "till death do us part." But LDS doctrine contributes the thrilling capstone that the family unit need not end at death, that family ties formed in this life can be eternal. As Latter-day Saints we understand that the Lord opened a way for these associations to be everlasting. It would be a capricious God who would concoct a plan whereby his children come to earth, obtain a physical body, marry and mate, develop poignant, profound, and soul-satisfying emotional bonds only to learn that it is all limited to a few short years of earth life, that there is no provision for carrying these relationships into the eternities. How senseless that would be, the worst possible ending to an otherwise remarkable plan! The death of a loved one would indeed be tragic and final.

What a lie Satan has foisted upon the world! No wonder the Lord saw fit to restore the gospel in our day, if for no other purpose than to bring back the true perspective on marriage and family life. And The Church of Jesus Christ of Latter-day Saints is the only religion making the "grand connection" between this life and eternity. The gospel of Jesus Christ boldly declares that the atonement of the Savior not only promises our resurrection from the grave with a restoration of our full faculties in a tangible body of flesh and bone (not blood) but also the potential of eternal family associations. Such a message should thrill the soul of anyone who has ever been in love, who has ever experienced the heart-pounding emotion and feelings of devotion for a spouse and children. What an inspiring backdrop it gives to dating, marriage, and the privilege of being a mother or father!

A number of LDS sayings exist as a commentary on this theme: "As man now is, God once was; as God now is, man may become"; " 'heaven' is a continuation of all that is good and wholesome about family life"; "the highest of celestial realms is unattainable alone"; "exalted beings continue in the family unit"; "to be resurrected without family would be 'hell' indeed."

As Church members we have a strong desire to comply with the laws of the gospel to insure our family continuation in the hereafter. Accepting the gospel commits us to regard marriage and parenting as central priorities in our lives. Elder Bruce R. McConkie wrote:

From the moment of birth into mortality to the time we are married in the temple, everything we have in the whole gospel system is to prepare and qualify us to enter that holy order of matrimony which makes us husband and wife in this life and in the world to come.

Then from the moment we are sealed together . . . everything connected with revealed religion is designed to help us keep the terms and conditions of our marriage covenant, so that this covenant will have efficacy, virtue, and force in the life to come. . . .

There is nothing in this world as important as the creation and perfection of family units . . . contemplated in the gospel of Jesus Christ. ("Salvation Is a Family Affair," *Improvement Era*, June 1970, pp. 43–44.)

From this lofty perspective, it is clear why prophet-leaders have given such high priority to family life. "No other success can compensate for failure in the home" (David O. McKay, *Improvement Era*, June 1964, p. 445). "The most important work you will ever do will be within the walls of your own home" (Harold B. Lee, *Stand Ye in Holy Places* [Salt Lake City: Deseret Book Company, 1974], p. 255). "Our success [as a people, as a Church] will largely be determined by how faithfully we focus on living the gospel in the home" (Spencer W. Kimball, *Ensign*, May 1979, p. 83). President Ezra Taft Benson has stated, "No other institution can take the place of the home or fulfill its essential function" ("The Values by Which to Live," *Leaders Magazine*, Oct.-Nov. 1984, p. 154).

The Church exists to complement the home. It provides a larger environment for family members to socialize with others and to worship, to receive gospel instruction and basic priesthood ordinances. The chance to develop individual character through leadership and service to others is an important opportunity available through the Church organization. Its facilities provide an opportunity for boys and girls with similar beliefs and backgrounds to fellowship with each other and allow, at the proper time, the dating and courtship process to occur. Temples, with sacred, impressive settings, are provided to unite couples and families together in the patriarchal order of the priest-hood. God sent angels to the earth to restore this sacred authority—available only through ordinances performed in the Lord's house.

Our efforts to reach out to "inactives" and nonmember friends (who misunderstand our enthusiasm) are rooted in a sincere desire to share the truth that families can be eter-nal. All who are honest in heart love their companions and children. They too can enjoy these blessings when there is proper instruction, commitment to principle, good works, and ordinances—but only then. We send missionaries throughout the world to declare this exciting message. As the Church continues its international thrust, the eternal nature of the family will be the common thread that will appeal to individuals in every country and culture.

Sacred Doctrines About the Family

The Prophet Joseph Smith taught the revolutionary idea that

> God himself was once as we are now, and is an exalted man, and sits enthroned in yonder heavens! That is the great secret. If the veil were rent today, and the great God who holds this world in its orbit . . . was to make himself visible . . . you would see him like a man in form—like yourselves in all the person, image, and very form as a man; for Adam was created in the very fashion, image and likeness of God . . . and conversed with him, as one man talks and com-munes with another.
>
> . . . It is the first principle of the Gospel to know for a cer-tainty the Character of God, and to know that we may con-verse with him as one man converses with another, and that he was once a man like us; yea, that God himself, the Father of us all, dwelt on an earth, the same as Jesus Christ himself did. (Joseph Smith, *Teachings of the Prophet Joseph Smith*, sel. Joseph Fielding Smith [Salt Lake City: Deseret Book Com-pany, 1938], pp. 345–6.)

The First Presidency of the Church, in a proclamation dated November 1909, proclaimed:

Man is the child of God, formed in the divine image and endowed with divine attributes, and even as the infant son of an earthly father and mother is capable in due time of becoming a man, so the undeveloped offspring of celestial parentage is capable, by experience through ages and aeons, of evolving into a God. (*Messages of the First Presidency*, comp. James R. Clark, vol. 4 [Salt Lake City: Bookcraft, 1970], p. 206.)

They further declared:

The doctrine of the pre-existence . . . pours a wonderful flood of light upon the otherwise mysterious problem of man's origin. It shows that man, as a spirit, was begotten and born of heavenly parents, and reared to maturity in the eternal mansions of the Father, prior to coming upon the earth in a temporal body. . . . It teaches that all men existed in the spirit before any man existed in the flesh, and that all who have inhabited the earth since Adam have taken bodies and become souls in like manner. (Ibid., p. 205.)

We are not, therefore, related to God as a vessel is to the potter, but as lineal offspring of the God of Heaven! ''I am a child of God'' is a literally true statement.

Joseph Smith explained that God created the earth as a stage in the development and refinement of his children. Heavenly parents send us, their spirit children, into a fallen world, where good and evil can exist together. That was not possible in our premortal existence. We came here to experience for ourselves the difference between right and wrong and to kindle in our souls, outside the presence of heavenly beings, a love of light and truth. For us to mature spiritually, and with the endowments of the physical flesh, it was essential that we be schooled in a mortal probation where very important insights and lessons prepare and qualify us for eternal privileges. Here, in this setting, we make choices and then experience the consequences that flow from obedience or rejection of natural and spiritual laws. The atonement of the Savior clears us of mistakes we make during our schooling process, if we sincerely repent and forsake our sins.

In the premortal life we saw Lucifer and his followers

banished when they rebelled against God and his plan. Since then they have dedicated themselves to impeding this plan in all ways possible to them. God uses our mortal conditions to expose us to and try us against the eternal opposites that exist. To keep our "second estate," mortality, we adhere to exacting principles of righteousness in the face of alternatives—the same straight and narrow way as followed by those who have gained exaltation before us. This is the pathway to eternal life. We learn correct principles as we obey eternal laws (D&C 88:34–36, 38–39). By coming to earth under these conditions we reconfirm to ourselves that the gospel of Jesus Christ *is* the safe, time-proven, reliable way to achieve eternal happiness, so that never in all of the eternities ahead will we rebel against truth as many of our spirit brothers and sisters once did.

Here we again confront Satan in his arguments and sophistries, many of them dealing with marriage and family living; but now we are in a setting foreign to our first estate, and we must again be willing to reject his ideas. Our lives become, as Alma declared, "a probationary state; . . . a time to prepare for that endless state . . . which is after the resurrection of the dead" (Alma 12:24).

As Parents, We Have a Similar Plan

In mortality, as parents, we imitate this heavenly pattern in our own homes. We willingly bear and rear our children, make sacrifices for them, and teach them about life, and provide the basic necessities for them. But if they are healthy and normal and still want to live in our home beyond a reasonable age (twenty-five? thirty?), we become a little anxious. We, like parents everywhere, want them to move out into the world, on their own; to marry, and to leave father and mother, to gain their own independence, and to rear the next generation. We want them to learn for themselves what we and others have tried to teach them but which can be gained only through experience. They must feel for themselves the challenges, the joy of righteous living, the responsible use of agency, the value of self-discipline, and the consequences of right decisions.

As parents we desire that our children seek good and resist evil of their own volition, not because we are controlling or forcing them. We want them to learn through their own trials that the gospel is the path to happiness. It is schooling of the highest order—the curriculum fashioned by mortal and divine tutelage. As parents we do our best to prepare our offspring for maturity, and to appreciate the God-ordained life cycle through which we all pass in our quest for exaltation. Brigham Young explained:

> There never was a time when there were not Gods and worlds, and when men were not passing through the same ordeals that we are now passing through. . . . You cannot comprehend this, but when you can, it will be to you a matter of great consolation. . . .
>
> The creations of God—the worlds that are and the worlds that have been,—who can grasp in the vision of his mind the truth that there never has been a time when there have not been worlds like this, and that there never will be a time when there will not be worlds organized and prepared for intelligent beings to dwell upon? (Brigham Young, *Discourses of Brigham Young*, sel. John A. Widtsoe [Salt Lake City: Deseret Book Company, 1941], pp. 22–23, 48.)

What a sacred trust heavenly parents confirm on mortals in sending their children—immortal spirit children —here to the earth to be reared by us, who are fallen, fallible, individuals! Yet children enrich the lives of parents as the parents prepare the children for adulthood. This plan provides both parent and child an opportunity to develop the very attributes of God—patience, charity, kindness, mercy, justice, love, and similar divine traits.

A Physical Body

In this life, we acquire a physical, earthly body which allows us privileges that we could not, apparently, have as spirits (D&C 138:50). We can, with this mortal body, marry, and then fashion other bodies through procreative powers. This life, therefore, becomes a foundation, the commencement, for an eternal kingdom and dominion. It is in this area of family life that Satan was damned. Satan was denied any family privileges. He and his followers were unworthy to receive a physical body with an endowment to marry and bear offspring. That was his great punishment—to be deprived of any experience with family life. What would he do with any children he was granted? No wonder fallen spirit beings are determined to prevent us from making eternal covenants and carrying procreative powers beyond this life! They want us to be limited eternally in the same way they are. Hence, they attempt to destroy us. Orson Pratt explained the principle:

> Could wicked and malicious beings, who have eradicated every feeling of love from their bosoms, be permitted to propagate their species, the offspring would partake of all the evil, wicked, and malicious nature of their parents. . . . *It is for this reason that God will not permit the fallen angels to multiply:* it is for this reason that God has ordained marriages for the righteous only; it is for this reason that God will put a final stop to the multiplication of the wicked after this life: it is for this reason that none but those who have kept the celestial law will be permitted to multiply after the resurrection: . . . for they alone are prepared to beget and bring forth [such] offspring. (*The Seer*, Oct. 1853, pp. 157–58; emphasis added.)

Perhaps one of the most profound reasons why we must strengthen our marriages and parenting abilities is centered in the truth that our time on earth to obtain a body, learn self-government, prove ourselves valiant and loyal to eternal principles, marry, and rear our posterity is very brief. We must be careful not to yield to temptations which may distract us from our goals.

Here We Choose an Eternal Companion

It is in this sphere that we select a companion, an eternal partner. In marriage, a couple is authorized to use their sexual powers to express their love and to bring other spirit children of the Father to earth. Family members who prove themselves valiant and faithful during their mortal probation are assured of eternal ties with each other in the patriarchal family of the Father. That is the ultimate goal of Latter-day Saints. Marriage is a critical phase in our schooling process.

> Verily I say unto you, that whoso forbiddeth to marry is not ordained of God, for marriage is ordained of God unto man. Wherefore, it is lawful that he should have one wife, and they twain shall be one flesh, and all this that the earth might answer the end of its creation; and that it might be filled with the measure of man, according to his creation before the world was made. (D&C 49:15–17.)

The Lord explained that women assist him in the great work of redeeming his children through marriage:

> For [a wife is] given unto [her husband] to multiply and replenish the earth, according to my commandment, and to fulfill the promise which was given by my Father before the foundation of the world, and for their exaltation in the eternal worlds, that they may bear the souls of men; for herein is the work of my Father continued, that he may be glorified. (D&C 132:63.)

No wonder we have a serious interest in dating, courting, moral cleanliness, marriage, and parenting. In this dimension of eternity, we have the opportunity to organize an eternal kingdom.[1]

Great care and prayerful preparation should accompany this undertaking. President Spencer W. Kimball once wrote:

> Marriage is perhaps the most vital of all the decisions and has the most far-reaching effects, for it has to do not only with immediate happiness, but eternal joys as well.
>
> In selecting one's companion for life and for eternity, cer-

---

1. Those who die before marriagable age, those who through no fault of their own never marry, and those worthy of eternal life whose spouses will not gain exaltation, will have this blessing made available to them at some future time.

tainly the most careful planning and thinking and praying
and fasting should be done *to be sure that of all the decisions,
this one is not wrong.* (*Ensign*, Nov. 1978, p. 103, emphasis
added.)

For us to extend family life beyond this sphere, much
depends on the decisions and actions we implement in our
earthly state. Orson Pratt stated:

> God . . . has ordained that the highest order and class of
> beings that should exist in the eternal worlds should exist in
> the capacity of husbands and wives, and that they alone
> should have the privilege of propagating their species. . . .
> Now it is wise, no doubt, in the Great Creator to thus limit
> this great and heavenly principle to those who have arrived
> or come to the highest state of exaltation, . . . to dwell in His
> presence, that they by this means shall be prepared to bring
> up their spirit offspring in all pure and holy principles in the
> eternal worlds, in order that they may be made happy. Con-
> sequently, He does not entrust this privilege of multiplying
> spirits with the terrestrial or telestial, or the lower order of
> beings there, nor with angels. But why not? Because they
> have not proved themselves worthy of this great privilege.
> (*Journal of Discourses* 13:186.)

As Latter-day Saints, we have a deep and abiding
interest in the progress of families—both within the
Church and in society at large. As sons and daughters of
God, we can best develop our godlike potential in an
environment of free choice, in which opportunities to live
the principles of the gospel of Jesus Christ are available.
When society is wicked, families are adversely influenced
and affected. When society maintains both a political
climate and a level of righteousness conducive to the Spirit
of the Lord, the Lord's plan is carried out more effectively.

Establishing an Eternal Family

2

Most of us want to know more than simply *what* is required on our part to gain eternal life; we want to know *why* we are to do what we do—we want what I call "perspective." If we understand the "why," or the theory behind something, then the "how," or the practice, seems to come more easily, more as a freewill offering. Since eternal life and the privilege of continuing family associations beyond this life is a primary goal for me, as I assume it is for you, let us look briefly at what the Lord expects of each of us if we are to establish an eternal family.

First, *we must understand and commit ourselves to the principles of the gospel of Jesus Christ.* That sounds obvious at first, but it is quite profound and represents a lifetime quest. Joseph Smith restored the gospel to enable us to learn how we may gain immortality and exaltation. For example, the Prophet explained the three most important truths which are essential to our understanding our own identity and relationship to the Godhead. They include the knowledge of (1) our Heavenly Father as the literal father of our spirit bodies; (2) the mission and role of Jesus Christ

as the Son of God, the Savior of the world, the great
Jehovah—a separate and distinct being from the Father;
and (3) the Holy Ghost as a male personage of spirit,
presently unembodied—a personal revelator and witness
to the truth of this latter-day work to each baptized
member of the Church and those earnestly seeking gospel
truth.

The Prophet clarified other theological concepts dealing
with our pre-earth life, the purpose of our mortal
probation, and our post-earth destiny. He explained the
purpose and sanctity of marriage and family relations as it
relates here and hereafter. He explained the first principles
of the gospel and testified to the reality of the Atonement
and the Resurrection. He brought into focus, through the
visitation of heavenly ministers, temple ordinances and
instruction, and specific knowledge and priesthood keys
which enable us to prepare for a celestial order of life. With
the restoration of this perspective, we may now carry out
our earthly probation knowing whom we worship and
how to worship him in an appropriate and intelligent
manner (D&C 93:19).

Second, *we need priesthood ordinances and covenants.*
Mortals seeking eternal life (with the exception of little
children and those with severe mental handicaps) must
receive priesthood ordinances that are essential to gain
membership in the Church and eventual exaltation. Baptism and temple marriage are two examples. It is through
priesthood ordinances and personal covenants that we
gain the understanding and spiritual power to live in a
world of wickedness and yet not be contaminated by its
influence.

Third, *we must become Christlike by incorporating into our
souls the very character and attributes of Deity.* ''Therefore,
what manner of men ought ye to be?'' Jesus asked the
Nephites. He then answered his own query, ''even as I
am.'' (3 Nephi 27:27.) There are many attributes mentioned in the scriptures that must become second nature to
us: charity, kindness, gentleness, compassion, mercy,
meekness, forgiveness, humility, patience, long-suffering

—to name a few. What marriage or parent-child relationship would not prosper with the liberal use of these qualities?

Of course, this is the really tough one for us—translating gospel principles into charitable actions. Mortality has a way of testing us in these attributes. Everyday living crowds in around us and chokes off our eternal perspective. There are many irritants and frustrations that accompany daily living. We forget so easily, it seems, our divine heritage and mission. Like Laman and Lemuel, who had numerous spiritual experiences and yet did not profit from them, we too can be overwhelmed by mortal distractions. Even Nephi and Lehi became discouraged on occasion in spite of the fact that they had been to the mountain top and seen great visions of the future. Our very mettle is tested through this mortal experience to see if we can develop the kind of life God lives.

Mortality has reduced us all to beings with immense shortcomings and inadequacies. However, even as weak mortals, we can be valiant servants when strengthened by obedience to gospel principles and the Spirit. But we must retain our perspective of the plan of salvation through a consistent program of gospel study, personal prayer, and service to others if we are to stay sharp and maintain a level of spirituality equal to our task. Table 2.1 illustrates the connection between our understanding basic gospel truths and our gaining the desire to conform to the plan and to develop a Christlike character, which leads to exaltation.

As we further our understanding of gospel truths (some examples of basics are given), we desire to be valiant sons and daughters of God because we understand our spiritual heritage and our purpose for mortality. We have ''no more disposition to do evil, but to do good continually'' (Mosiah 5:2). We are, to use Alma's words, ''born of God'' (Alma 5:14). As the plan of salvation becomes alive for us, we become more Christlike and see the importance of treating each other as literal brothers and sisters traveling the same journey. *Our treatment of*

Table 2.1

OUR SPIRITUAL PERSPECTIVE CAN LEAD US TO EXALTATION

When we understand that:	Then we desire to:	Which leads to our becoming:	Which leads to exaltation
We have heavenly parents	Please God and serve each other	Christlike	Sanctification
We lived before this life as their spirit children	Follow correct principles and obey the commandments	Charitable	Eternal marriage
We are all, therefore, literal brothers and sisters	Communicate with our Father in prayer	Unselfish	Eternal increase
Mortality is a way to test and develop our character	Search the scriptures for help	Kind	Eternal life
We make mistakes—we are all fallen beings	Follow the living prophets	Gentle	
Jesus suffered and died for our sins	Gain the Spirit of the Lord	Compassionate	
Satan is a brother determined to destroy us—he is here on this earth	Receive priesthood ordinances	Merciful	
We need inspiration from the Holy Ghost	Enter into sacred covenants with God our Father	Meek	
We need counsel from living prophets	Be a valiant servant of the Lord	Forgiving	
We need scriptures to understand the gospel	Cleanse ourselves of sin, of past mistakes that interfere with our service and mission	Humble	
We need priesthood ordinances and covenants with our Father	Be whole and pure before God	Patient	
	Live by every word of the Lord		

The Path to Damnation and Stagnation

If we do not comprehend:	Then we remain:	Which leads to eternal limitations
The purpose of mortality	Selfish	Immortality only
The character and personality of God and our relationship to him	A "natural man"	Being separate and single forever
The need for a Savior	An "enemy to God" and his work	Inability to be sanctified by law
The effects of sin	Carnal, sensual	
Spiritual laws of progress	Careless and indifferent to spiritual matters	
The spiritual heritage of man	Low in self-esteem	
	Insensitive to others	
	Temperamental	
	Unable to love others	

others is commensurate with our comprehension of the gospel.
Gospel truths, together with a witness of the Holy Ghost,
humble and soften the heart, and we can more easily
overlook faults and failings and clear up our own mistakes.
We are not easily offended by the actions of others. When
we genuinely love others, working together in harmony
and unity to achieve mutual goals is much easier. We
behave more charitably because we have developed the
attributes of the Savior.

It sounds reasonable and simple, doesn't it? But it is not
easy to put into practice, because of our fallen natures and
our struggles with the flesh, which cry out for attention.
However, we can grow in our capacity for self-discipline
and the ability to reach out and bless others, to be unselfish.

The lower portion of table 2.1 illustrates how we may
destroy personal relationships or not allow them to mature
to any extent. When we are ignorant of basic gospel truths,
our view of the meaning of life is shallow or nonexistent. If
sin has blunted our spiritual sensitivity or if the interests of
the world have superseded our spiritual values, we then
lose our eternal perspective and, as King Benjamin explained, we become a "natural man" (Mosiah 3:19). The
natural man's perspective and actions are self-centered.
He functions barely above the animal plane. He seeks his
own ends and has little charity. Rather, he may use good
behavior only as a deception to exploit or as a means of
manipulation for selfish gain.

President Spencer W. Kimball explained that "every
divorce is the result of selfishness on the part of one or the
other or both parties to a marriage contract" (*Marriage,*
[Salt Lake City: Deseret Book Company, 1979], p. 42; used
by permission). Table 2.1 presents the rationale that selfishness is rooted in a lack of spiritual knowledge. Why
would one insincerely commit oneself to principles or
make personal promises that are meaningless? Such a
condition leads to impaired relationships and to behavior
incompatible with a celestial order. One becomes spiritually undisciplined and ungovernable, thereby failing to

meet the requirements of celestial law (D&C 88:34–35, 39–40). Unto such people the final judgment brings restricted glory.

No Immunity to Family Challenges

Despite the fact that we "know" all this as Church members, we still cannot relax our vigilance over our families. Though we know what is right, we still find it difficult to achieve. This relates to three areas.

1. Since God has granted mankind free agency in a wicked world, some will choose evil. Ever since Eve partook of the forbidden fruit, Satan has continued his efforts to make evil appear good. When children reach a level of maturity, they may, in spite of our best efforts to train them otherwise, choose evil and exercise their agency contrary to our wishes or their own self-interest. As long as agency exists there is the chance that individuals may select unwisely and cut themselves off from blessings to which they are otherwise entitled. (We learned that lesson in the premortal life.) God allows evil to exist here. It is a part of our probation. But it is our personal choice as to whether we embrace it. The more wicked the world grows, the greater the enticement to choose evil becomes. Opposition is part of this mortal plan to test our resolve to be righteous. Alcohol and cigarette advertisements, along with the pleasing portrayal of immorality in our day, are designed by conspiring men to look sophisticated and attractive. (See D&C 89:4.) Many succumb to these allurements.

Both Satan and man are responsible for the evil here, and God permits it because without temptation man would not have agency (see D&C 29:39) (remember that Satan was cast out to this earth for such a purpose). But the Lord has done something about this evil. The Savior took upon himself the sins of the world. He did this because free agency was a necessary part of our growth. Since we must have agency in order to move forward, Christ personally suffered the punishment for those wrong choices for which we are truly sorry and which we take steps to change.

History provides many examples of wayward children that came from good homes. Friends, social pressures, and our media can exercise a negative influence on all of us. Even conscientious parents make mistakes. After all, this is the first time in all eternity that we have had the opportunity to be parents. Surely in the learning-to-be-parents process, we make our share of errors and misjudgments. We may be too strict or too lenient; we must be somewhat philosophical about that to remain sane! Unfortunately, many parents spend their lives berating themselves for their children's errant ways if the children made choices contrary to the values they were taught. In such cases, the children will be held responsible for their own sins.

Where children go astray, parents must never give up hope. We never know when the lessons of life will teach a wayward son or daughter lessons that we were unable to convey. The experience of the prodigal son occurs with some regularity in our own day.

2. Perhaps we have not drunk deeply from the "gospel well" ourselves and shared the Restoration with our children on a consistent basis. Could any Church member honestly say: "You mean we are supposed to hold a weekly meeting with our family to instruct them? What would we do? I've never heard of that before." We may be lifelong, "active" members of the Church and yet have had no more than a superficial brush with its doctrines. Have we personally searched the scriptures as the Savior enjoined? to any depth? The purpose of life, the mission of Christ, the importance of modern revelation and living prophets may never have been unveiled to us—nor have we sought it—sufficiently to pass it on to our offspring. Elder John A. Widtsoe commented, "It is a paradox that men will gladly devote time every day for many years to learn a science or an art; yet will expect to win a knowledge of the gospel, which comprehends all sciences and arts, through perfunctory glances at books or occasional listening to sermons." (*Evidences and Reconciliations: Three*

Volumes, G. Homer Durham, arr. [Salt Lake City: Bookcraft, 1960], p. 16.)

If our level of gospel scholarship has been so superficial that we have not felt the excitement and revelation that accompanies diligent study and makes us want to share these great truths with our children, they will not be excited about them either. They, of course, hear bits and pieces of the gospel and gain the false impression that they are well informed—or they seek answers to the "mysteries" without being grounded in the fundamentals. (Seminary and institute teachers see this problem routinely.) Busy schedules may crowd out gospel study. Also, heavy-handed expounding of Church doctrine is sometimes imposed on children without any sensitivity to their learning readiness or mental age.

The worldliness of our modern society doesn't help either. We are flooded with advertisements for technological gadgets, cars, clothing, and entertainment. Television is often a greater source of information and influence on our children's values and life-style than we are. Time for honest, deep searching and reflection on gospel principles may be lacking. Family home evenings, family councils, and family prayer are nonexistent or too infrequently used for discovering the "pearl of great price." Sabbath days may be wasted in activities that do not contribute to faith and spirituality. We may act as though attending a three-hour block once a week is sufficient to build great faith in the heart of man.

If we are not actively sharing the gospel with others, we see little need to "pay the price" of serious gospel study. (There is a real key—to involve ourselves in missionary work. Then the entire gospel comes alive! On the other hand, returned missionaries who do not continue using their skills may think they already know all there is to know about the gospel from their twenty-four-month stint.) Check yourself on this right now. How familiar are *you* with the characters, background, structure, events, and story of the Book of Mormon (beyond 2 Nephi), the Doctrine and Covenants, or the Pearl of Great Price? These records contain powerful voices for our day. Evaluate your own gospel scholarship. How well acquainted are you with the ministry and travels of Paul, the life of the Master on both continents, the message of the Old Testament prophets—and can you locate their writings?

Though we need not be doctrinal scholars, few of us are familiar enough with these sacred writings to be able to help our families become familiar with them. The Lord indicated his disappointment with those who "treat . . . lightly the things [scriptures] you have received" (D&C 84:54). The Lord counseled parents: "And again, inasmuch as parents have children . . . that teach them not to understand the doctrine of repentance, faith in Christ the Son of the living God, and of baptism and the gift of the Holy Ghost, . . . *the sin be upon the heads of the parents*" (D&C 68:25; emphasis added).

When the home is not *the* gospel learning center, worldly values take precedence. The Lord explained the danger: "their hearts are set so much upon the things of this world" (D&C 121:35; emphasis added).

3. We may fail to establish a close, personal, relationship with each member of our family. Even when we understand the basic principles of the gospel, transmitting them to the next generation requires an environment of love and acceptance. It is difficult to influence children without a close, personal relationship with each one. Consider your own family. First, your spouse. Are you two getting better at being companions? Are you falling more "in love" with each other as time passes? Are you united in your goals for your family? Are you loving? affectionate? A colleague shared with me an incident of a man who told his bishop, "I would like to divorce my wife so that I can go on a mission and serve the Lord." Stunned, the bishop asked for an explanation. "She has been such a pain to me all of our married life. I would like to get rid of her and go out and serve the Lord." The man had forgotten the perspective Paul gave that neither the man nor the woman is acceptable before the Lord without the other (1 Corinthians 11:11).

Consider the relationship you have with each of your children. Which child is the most lovable? the hardest to express your affection to? Do your children seek counsel from you? Are they at ease around you? too casual? What motivation is there for them to want to marry in the temple based on the example you and your spouse have set? Are you able to express your love frequently and spontaneously to each of them? Do they reciprocate? Is your relationship with them strained and awkward?

Let's test your charity right now for your children. As a father, if you invited a married couple in your neighborhood over for a piece of cake and a glass of milk, and the husband spilled his drink all over the tablecloth and your carpet, how would you react? Would you jump up excitedly, grab a spoon and thump him on the forehead, saying, "What are you doing to my carpet?" (You would certainly get his attention if you did that!) No, most husbands would probably calmly respond with, "No problem, Bill. We will take care of that." But if one of our children has a similar accident, we think he has been planning to do it for weeks and we are ready to "excommunicate" him from the family table. (Perhaps we ought to treat our children at least as well as we do the neighbors. After all, we have invited our children to spend eternity with us; the neighbors are simply over for some cake and milk.)

When we fail to strengthen our family relationships, we set ourselves up for crises—usually when the children are teenagers. Here is an important principle in parenting: You cannot positively influence your children (or spouse) unless you first establish a relationship with them. You must pay the price in time, love, patience, and tenderness. They must know that you care about them. Any other approach is foolhardy. (Helps will be given in later chapters.)

The Gospel and Relationship Skills

Some of us have more difficulty developing good relationships than others. If we grew up in a home in which commitment to Christian principles was less than adequate or in which relationship skills were poorly modeled, we may be somewhat handicapped in knowing how to develop close family ties, or how to make positive changes. Unfortunately, instead of humbly seeking ways to improve, we often become defensive and excuse our poor performances rather than seeking to become more proficient. We can change. Though we may have to work harder than others by humbling ourselves and then gathering ideas from the scriptures, articles, and books, we can improve as companions and parents. We have an important investment in doing so.

Here is the good news. In general, we already possess these skills and abilities sufficiently to succeed. We have been practicing them day in and day out all our lives. In our growing years we learned that in order to "get along" socially and to be compatible with others, we had to be pleasant and conversational to some extent. Think about it. We do know how to be kind, mannerly, sweet, and patient—on the golf course, or with strangers, or with customers who might make a purchase. Surely if we convinced a partner to marry us, we must have some pretty good communication skills! (Unless we got a mail-order bride.)

I often suggest to husbands and wives that if they were to divorce and begin dating again, both would manifest pleasant and charming personality traits and adequate social skills with any *new* dating partner. They are already equipped with enough skills to deal socially with others. "So, why not change the way you relate with each other now and save yourself a lot of trouble? It will be a lot cheaper and you have so much invested in each other already." Yes, I am convinced we do possess the necessary ability—when we want to use it. The problem is that when we have a history of hurting each other in a relationship, when our hearts are hardened, when we have lost the Spirit, we do not use the skills we possess. But, *it is our motivation or lack of spirituality that is at fault, not our skill level.*

Most of us communicate quite well when we desire to; not so well when we are angry or agitated. When we are angry with one of the kids or our spouse and the telephone rings, we certainly don't use the same angry voice with the caller that we were just using with a family member. Suddenly, we are pleasant, warm, and wonderful. We really do have the necessary communication skills when we are in a "good mood," when we want to be.

The home is the great university in which we teach, learn, model, and practice human relations. Sometimes in that sacred setting, however, we are the most shabby in our application of Christian principles. Marriage counselors and Church leaders see individuals who are efficient in running business enterprises or Church auxiliaries, or priesthood units, but who are unable to extend the same courtesies to those of their own household. Why is it we can be so different in public than in private? Ought we not to be genuine regardless of the situation we are in?

Marital happiness does not come by chance, biorhythms, astrological signs, or megavitamins, but rather as the result of healthy interaction between people who love each other. It comes when primary human needs such as love and worth are reaffirmed on a consistent, ongoing basis; when problem solving is approached with mutual love and respect for each other's opinions. Charity is the mantle that must cover all family events, for it is there we forge, develop, strengthen, and mature bonds of love; or stifle, blunt, and perhaps destroy them.

Before proceeding to the next chapter, take a moment to review the following list, "My Quest for Eternal Life." Consider each of the items carefully.

My Quest for Eternal Life: A Review

Instructions: Please answer the following questions privately and then, as a couple, share your answers.

1. Who am I really? What is the origin of my mortal body? my spirit body?

2. What are at least five important reasons I am here on this earth?

3. Why is free agency such an important element of progression in this life? What is the relationship between free agency and keeping the commandments of God?

4. Comment to yourself on this statement: The sum of the gospel is family relations.

5. How important is marriage in the overall plan of life? Why? What does it mean to be "sealed" to someone? What is my favorite scripture on marriage?

6. If I project my temple marriage beyond this life, what are my possibilities? What might I be doing a thousand years from now?

7. Why is the power of procreation given to me in mortality? What are the rules God has laid down concerning the use of these powers?

8. How do my children relate to me in this life? in eternity? What is their relationship to God? What does he expect of me in rearing his children?

9. Who is Satan? What are his motives? Why was he cast out of our premortal state? What was his real punishment?

10. Why does the Lord have us make covenants with him? What covenants have I made with him concerning family relations?

11. I have been given the right to revelation from the Lord. Am I receiving impressions and inspiration? Am I growing in my ability to understand spiritual principles? in my ability to strengthen my family members?

12. To remain married and continue procreative powers beyond this life, what must I do to reach exaltation? (See D&C 131:1–4.) Why? What happens in the other degrees of glory concerning marriage and family life? (See D&C 132:17.)

13. Is the Lord pleased with my performance as a husband or wife? as a parent?

14. How does the atonement of the Savior fit into my life? my marriage? my family relations? Can I repent (apologize) easily when I make a mistake or offend?

15. What attributes do I lack in being a more charitable companion? father or mother?

16. How do I show love and charity to members of my own family? Is my partner my best friend? Are we compatible? deeply in love?

17. Do I express my love to each of my family members? When did I last do so?

18. Am I using this life for the purposes the Lord had in mind when he sent me here? Do I have my patriarchal blessing? Do I read it often? What are my strengths? my weaknesses?

19. Since I have been married in the temple, what happens when I die and go to the spirit world? What is the status of my marriage then? in the resurrection?

20. Would my spouse marry me if he or she had it to do over again? Are my children happy that I am their parent? Why don't I go and ask them?

Building a
Strong Marriage

3

A general maxim in family relations says that "as the marriage goes, so goes the family." Marriage is the most important relationship in the family constellation, not only for the personal growth and development of each spouse but also because it becomes the basic model from which children learn about their own sex roles and how to relate to the opposite sex. There are a number of important reasons why we need to build strong marriages, particularly as Latter-day Saints.

Personal Happiness

As Americans, we seem bent on pursuing happiness regardless of the path to it. We regard marriage as a primary source of happiness:

> The most popular—and the roughest—contact sport in the country is not professional football; it is marriage. Consider the statistics: Over 90 percent of us try our hand at it, either ignoring the dangers or simply hoping for the best. A third of us, however, sustain so many injuries that we are

willing to suffer the humiliation of divorce to get off the field. Yet, the promise, the attractiveness, is so great that 80 percent of those divorced put themselves back into marriage —most of them within three years. Clearly, the problem is not how to make matrimony more popular; it's how to make it less hazardous. (Carlfred Broderick, *Couples* [New York City: Simon and Schuster, 1979], p. 13.)

Whether marriage becomes "less hazardous" is rooted in two major factors: (1) personal righteousness and (2) the quality of marriage and family relationships.

Individual righteousness. Personal righteousness by way of keeping the commandments is a fundamental key to happiness. President Spencer W. Kimball taught that "no one, single or married, was ever sublimely happy unless he was righteous. There are temporary satisfactions and camouflaged situations for the moment, but permanent, total happiness can come only through cleanliness and worthiness." (*Marriage,* p. 47.)

One reason that happiness centers in righteousness is that when we obey God-given laws, we are acting in harmony with our divine nature as children of God. As we obey his commandments, we are conforming to eternal laws on which happiness is based. As Joseph Smith taught, "when we obtain any blessing from God, it is by obedience to that law upon which it is predicated" (D&C 130:21). What parent does not want his children to be happy? But we must abide the law. Lehi taught that "men are, that they might have joy" (2 Nephi 2:25). Alma counseled his son, "Wickedness never was happiness" (Alma 41:10).

Joseph Smith explained to the School of the Prophets that one element of faith included "an actual knowledge to any person, that the course of life which he pursues is according to the will of God, is essentially necessary to enable him to have that confidence in God without which no person can obtain eternal life" (comp. N. B. Lundwall, *Lectures on Faith* [Salt Lake City: Lundwall, n.d.], 6:2). The Holy Ghost confirms to our spirit feelings of divine approbation and spiritual wholeness as we obey law. The explanation continued by saying that without the knowledge that we are pleasing God, we would "grow weary in (our) minds, and faint" (ibid., 6:4).

The quality of marriage and family relations. The other major variable of personal happiness is tied to the quality of our marriage and our family relations. Marriage is designed to bring happiness and personal growth to each of us. Life, to be lived deeply and fully, requires the intimate union of a husband and wife who love each other and who are committed to each other's welfare. In the Lord's plan, "neither is the man without the woman, neither the woman without the man" (1 Corinthians 11:11). The challenges and crises of mortality can best be met with a companion who provides the therapy of a close friend within the context of marriage.

When we express love to family members and those feelings are reciprocated, there is a sense of personal fulfillment. In contrast, when a marriage is unhealthy and filled with strife and bickering, or when children are unruly and unmanageable, there are feelings of alienation, anger, and frustration. The Spirit of the Lord withdraws.

Quality family relations develop in a setting in which two people understand the profound commitment involved in an eternal relationship. Both are willing to forego selfish interests in order to benefit the partnership. Each is as concerned about his partner's happiness as he is with his own. Marriage works best when mature people are secure enough in their own personal makeup to enable them to reach out and contribute to the welfare of others.

Marital happiness depends on the degree to which our personal righteous goals are fulfilled in marriage. We experience personal growth, companionship, sexual and emotional intimacy, a sharing of personal thoughts and feelings, rearing children as a team, and confronting life with mutual optimism and confidence. These goals are the very fiber of quality family living. When we function well at home, we experience a sense of well-being, security, and personal satisfaction.

Individuals sometimes handicap themselves by marrying for the wrong reasons: to escape from a home environment, discouragement with school, boredom; the anticipation of a new status and the expectation that marriage will always be exciting; as a legal sexual outlet, or a cover-up for premarital pregnancy; feeling obligated to marry another person because of a "comfort level" of steady dating or pity for another human being; unrealistic expectations about marriage, and an immature perspective about the complexities of the real world. Often these individuals spend their lives trying to overcome the severe limitations that arise from these beginnings.

The first few years of marriage may be somewhat of a shock because dating does not, and cannot, prepare us adequately for marriage. One's true character is sometimes not apparent in the dating stage. We are too busy "faking each other out" and "being cool" to allow the differences in background and values to become obvious in the short run. Marginal mental health problems can be hidden during the excitement of dating and courting and surface only after marriage settles into reality and two people begin living day in and day out with each other.

Some have argued that this is reason enough to have two individuals live together before marriage, to become acquainted with these subtle personality differences before making any long-term commitments. The Lord wisely forbids that course and expects us to make our own careful preparation and then marry another who has acquired or is developing the character attributes of the Savior—love, charity, humility, understanding, forgiveness, patience, long-suffering, and similar virtues essential in relating well with others.

Whether we have acquired these attributes becomes apparent before long. The close intimacy of marriage calls for their application at the highest level. This is why those who marry in their teens generally face major obstacles in coping with the pressures and adjustments that naturally arise in the course of married life. Such individuals are usually unable to cope well with the demands that marriage makes. They simply have not gained the maturity they need to succeed in marriage.

This is one reason for the Lord's counsel to have every young man serve a mission before marriage. Through this service men learn many of the lessons which are so applicable to marriage—faith, leadership, service, humility, charity, sacrifice for others—and they acquire a testimony of the gospel. Much needed maturity is gained to help them prepare for the responsibilities of married life. We could solve many problems that are manifested in early marriages if boys would serve missions before matrimony. The ages of nineteen to twenty-five are crucial in the maturation process—particularly for young men. (Besides, after riding a ten-speed bike with a horrible seat for twenty-four months, they come home more humble and prepared for almost anything that life will throw at them.)

Those who are not happily married, and yet who are unwilling to divorce, often try to compensate for defects in the marriage by substituting for them work, hobbies, sports, clubs, children, or activities away from home. It is obvious, however, that there are no satisfying alternatives for the companionship of a healthy marriage. President Joseph F. Smith observed:

> There can be no genuine happiness separate and apart from the home, and every effort made to sanctify and preserve its influence is uplifting to those who toil and sacrifice for its establishment. Men and women often seek to substitute some other life for that of the home; they would make themselves believe that the home means restraint; that the highest liberty is the fullest opportunity to move about at will. There is no happiness without service, and there is no service greater than that which converts the home into a divine institution, and which promotes and preserves family life.
>
> Those who shirk home responsibilities are wanting in an important element of social well-being. They may indulge themselves in social pleasures, but their pleasures are superficial and result in disappointment later in life. The occupa-

tions of men sometimes call them from their homes; but the thought of home-coming is always an inspiration to well doing and devotion. . . . The strongest attachments of childhood are those that cluster about the home, and the dearest memories of old age are those that call up the associations of youth and its happy surroundings. (Joseph F. Smith, *Gospel Doctrine*, 5th ed. [Salt Lake City: Deseret Book Company, 1939], pp. 300–301.)

Too often unmarried people conclude: "I know I'll be happy once I am married," or, "Once I have children, then I will find real happiness," or, "Marriage will solve all my problems." The belief that marriage and becoming a parent will of themselves bestow happiness is rather naive. Such is not the case, of course, as any married person will attest, because happiness is not the result of acquiring marital roles. Marital happiness comes from being married to another person with similar values and goals and who is committed to work harmoniously toward common objectives. It is in meeting each other's companionship needs and understanding each other's heart— true intimacy—that genuine happiness abounds.

Parental happiness, by the same token, comes not from having children but from working together to rear them. It is a thrill to see children reflect the counsel of parents and others who love them and who have their best interest at heart. Children who return that love, who shoulder responsibility, who respond to wise counsel, who mirror the best of life—children who possess this maturity embody the very essence of parental joy. Parents are rewarded when their offspring establish strong marriages and healthy families of their own. Business failures, health problems, or other reverses, can be surmounted. But when children do not respond to parental counsel and guidance, or worse yet, when children are openly antagonistic towards parents who have labored many years to succor and rear them—such responses lead to heartbreak, estrangement, and disappointment. Little wonder that the investment we make to strengthen our marriage and increase the quality time we spend in relationship-building activities with children during their formative years will later pay great dividends. This is an obvious message from the Lord and the prophets as well as those who work in family relations: start early to establish close relationships with children, and carefully monitor those relationships over the years.

However, it is often in the early years of a child's development that the requirements of vocation or educational degrees make their greatest demand on dad's time. Men must be very careful and sensitive to the God-given priority of fathering, for children may never recover from a poor relationship with a father—or mother—during those critical years of their social and emotional development.

Companionship

Companionship is the most frequent response women give when asked why they marry. A woman anticipates exchanging ideas, thoughts, and feelings with her husband. The problem is that she often marries someone who won't talk to her. A rather common question of women to counselors is "How can I get my husband to talk to me?" Perhaps some culturally inhibiting factors operate to influence this problem. In general, boys are not trained in their formative years to express feelings and emotions openly. Perhaps the "macho" image best describes the problem. Boys grow up with the idea that it is "sissy" to cry or to let others know of any hurt, weakness, or disappointment. It is not "manly" to do so, or to be overly demonstrative about emotions. Somehow, sharing personal viewpoints and emotional responses is not the therapeutic experience for men that it usually is for women. But men must cultivate the opportunity to share in this way or they will miss out on an important dimension of life and be a frustration to their wives.

After spending the day with little ones, a wife may look forward to some adult conversation. However, her husband may be insensitive to her need, or he may consider his schedule and work day too mundane to review.

But couples need to process a great deal of information, matters essential to their marital and family well-being. Men, please be sensitive to your wife's need for both your head and your heart. Your wife ought to be your best friend and confidante. You two have a great deal to share, to discuss, to resolve. Though the events of the day may seem somewhat trivial to you, it is important that you share ideas, opinions, and feelings with your wife so that she can learn your views on life, work, and things that please you or cause you frustration. She can then improve as a wife and be an effective counselor-therapist. On the other hand, you need to know her views as a wife and helpmeet, and see her feminine perspective on home and family—if you are to be an effective husband-leader. Don't neglect her. Share your ideas and feelings with her frequently and ask her if you are meeting her needs for companionship. President Harold B. Lee once said:

> I say to you brethren the most dangerous thing that can happen between you and your wife is apathy . . . , for them to feel that we are not interested in their affairs, that we are not expressing our love and sharing our affection in countless ways. (Regional Representatives' seminar, 12 Dec. 1970.)

Wives, encourage your husbands to risk and share feelings and thoughts with you. (Sometimes, unknowingly perhaps, a wife may interrupt her husband when he does attempt to share personal matters, and he may become discouraged and retreat from risking or initiating intimate dialogue.) If you are not sure how well you are doing, ask your partner if your level of sharing is adequate in your marriage.

From a mental health standpoint, companionship provides an important service: *therapy.* This is one of the most important roles in marriage. In addition to sharing common information, the life cycle is filled with stress that will require the highest form of companionship if we are to survive. Consider the life cycle of a typical man.

Before marriage, you may wonder if you will ever

marry and you may even outwardly reconcile yourself to the possibility that you may remain single. But before you realize it, events bring you together with an attractive young woman and you date, "fall in love," court, marry, and begin your life as a husband. You learn about sexual intimacy, which has been off limits up to now. You now begin this sacred venture. Sexual intimacy can lead to pregnancy, for which neither partner is quite prepared. The next nine months are very interesting and educational. If you expect regular meals, you may have to dust off your old missionary cooking skills, since food has lost its appeal for her. When (and if) that tapers off, she begins to fill out. She may feel you don't love her and be jealous of all those skinny girls walking by, so you have to tell her ten times a day that you do love her. Pregnancy usually affects moods which sometimes makes sexual relations sporadic and uncomfortable; this requires charity and understanding on the part of each spouse.

Soon, however, the waiting is over. You go (quickly?) to the hospital, where your wife learns something about the "atonement," and passing through the "shadow of death." (A new mother can't believe, after ten hours of labor, that anybody would ever have more than one child!) Then, fortunately, after a "normal" delivery the hospital staff takes care of everything for the next three days, which is great for your wife. But it becomes too expensive to leave them there longer, so home they come. Now, the fun begins. The reality of being parents asserts itself rather rudely—with frequent nighttime feedings, diaper changes, and breath checks!

You learn as a husband, after the first child, that if your wife nurses, she will have to get up and take care of the noise that has disturbed your slumber. But if you use a bottle, you kick each other to see who will get up and do the feeding. Men are great fakers at this point, as every wife knows. "Who, what, I don't hear anything!" he mumbles as he rolls over and goes back to sleep. The wife's motherhood "guilt" takes over as the baby cries, and she gets up to take care of the newborn—cussing her husband for getting her pregnant but being unwilling to take much responsibility for the results.

As the life cycle moves ahead, your child is soon two years old—a very interesting species. Then he is in school. Meetings with the teachers begin. (They are not as thrilled with him as you thought they should be.) Then it's Cub Scouts, Pinewood Derby time, and time for him to receive the priesthood. One more year brings a teenager. Who ever invented them? I don't remember being that way when I was young.

Now, your hair begins to recede, change color, or leave you permanently. You find that you can't run up and down the basketball floor as you once did in high school. They have lengthened the size of the court, it seems. You need oxygen to make it through the first quarter. You need bifocals to read the phone book or the paper because your arm is not long enough. Meanwhile, "very close" veins strike your sweetheart, and staying up to see the New Year come in lost its appeal some time ago. Your teeth need recapping, and the twentieth year high school reunion is here. How could you have been out of high school that long?

After your child graduates from high school, you come up with money for college and a mission. (Somehow he never saved much toward either one.) Suddenly, it seems, you are saying good-bye in the MTC or airport, and your missionary is off to a new adventure (at least the Lord will know where he is, and you know how much your expenses will be). He finishes his mission, stumbles around for a while trying to decide on a career, then announces that the girl he has been dating so casually is to be his wife! You look at the "outlaws" and decide he could have done better, but he is old enough to make his own decisions.

On the way to his temple marriage you relax and figure that all your problems with this child are over. And, of course, you missed on that one too. You'll need to help them through school, give them a car, and help with the utilities. Then they announce that you are going to be a grandparent. That sounds great until you see that you have the baby every weekend because they are too cheap (poor) to get a babysitter, to say nothing of your own day-care center while your daughter-in-law works to put bread on the table.

By now your gallbladder is acting up. You find it difficult to sleep past 6:00 A.M. Your parents pass on, leaving you to be the senior citizens, and your body now feels the full effect of Adam's fall. Where did the time go? When you were twenty years old you thought that anyone who was forty could go at any time. Now sixty is beginning to look pretty decent! (You wouldn't go back and relive it again though, would you?)

Obviously, everyone needs his own live-in physician and therapist in order to make it safely and sanely through this life cycle. Your therapist, of course, should be—no, must be—your spouse. That is the great commitment and, it turns out, the joy of marriage—sharing hearts and feelings, meeting life head-on with the very soul with whom you have made eternal covenants. You mature together in the endowments of life, grateful to God for the journey you traveled together. Of course, challenges come along. That is what will bring the character traits essential to exaltation. What fun would life be without them to add spice, to test your ability to be compatible? You feel deeply the satisfaction of a life well lived and the triumph over the weakness of the flesh. You have come a long way in problem solving, decision making, and understanding each other's philosophy of life. That is the commitment we make when we marry. But, what do you know about marriage at nineteen? twenty? twenty-five? thirty? Luckily, the Lord allows us about fifty years together here to see if we can "put it together" for eternity, if we can become one. We agreed, didn't we, at marriage to accept each other's weaknesses as well as the strengths? We can't be "fair-weather" spouses any more than we can be "fair-weather" Latter-day Saints.

Too often, the following seems to be true:

Some married couples live very superficially together. They communicate about routine matters, but do not share their deepest thoughts. They live almost separate lives under one roof. They meet each other's elementary needs but never venture into what I call relationship-in-depth. Surprisingly enough, they may never even really get to know each other, because all they reveal is a limited area of their true selves. They simply live together on the basis of a mutual exchange of services. He "brings home the bacon," she takes care of the house, she gives him sex, he gives her children. Based on a few such elementary exchanges, the marriage soon becomes dull and dreary.

Such mediocre marriages are very common in our culture. Yet often these very people are tormented by the longing for a relationship that is richer, deeper, and more meaningful. They are love-starved, and often they turn in other directions to seek what marriage has failed to give them. The wife may become almost completely preoccupied with her children, the husband gets immersed in his job. Sharing life in depth with another person (your spouse in marriage) is the solution to most of our human problems. It is in loving and being loved that we do find the real meaning of life. (David Mace, *Getting Ready for Marriage* [Nashville: Abingdon Press, 1977], p. 68.)

The commitment of marriage is a covenant to share life, in-depth, together. Both must be therapeutic, good listeners, and healers of both psychological and physical wounds. After years of living together we should know more than anyone else how to love, bless, inspire, lift, strengthen, comfort, and bring joy to each other. Being self- and spouse-reliant in solving life's challenges is the task. A husband and wife should be the first and most effective line of defense for each other against the buffetings of the world.

Resolving problems is much easier when both keep the purposes of marriage and family uppermost in their minds and hearts. Learning to be great companions is the grand objective and reward of marriage. A deep and lasting friendship makes the journey of life much more pleasant.

Theological Reasons

Perhaps the most important reason to strengthen marriage and parenting practices centers in our theology. Most Church members are aware of the doctrine from section 76 of the Doctrine and Covenants that there are three degrees of glory to which we may be assigned. The first four verses of section 131 explain that those who gain the highest degree of glory within the celestial kingdom are the *only ones* who continue to possess the power of procreation following the resurrection. Section 132 adds that those who do not marry by the priesthood "cannot be enlarged, but remain separately and singly" through all eternity (v. 17). President Joseph Fielding Smith explained:

> Some will gain celestial bodies with all the powers of exaltation and eternal increase. . . .
> In both of these kingdoms [terrestrial and telestial, and even the lower portions of the celestial] there will be changes in the bodies and limitations. *They will not have the power of increase [posterity], neither the power or nature to live as husbands and wives, for this will be denied them and they cannot increase.* . . .
> Some of the functions in the celestial body will not appear in the terrestrial body, neither in the telestial body, and *the power of procreation will be removed.* (*Doctrines of Salvation*, comp. Bruce R. McConkie, 3 vols. [Salt Lake City: Bookcraft, 1954–56], 2:287–88; emphasis added.)

Can you fathom that—to lose the power *and* the nature to be married, along with the powers of procreation, that we treasure in this life? I know of no statement in the writings of the prophets or the scriptures that causes a more sober reflection on the meaning and purpose of our family life here on the earth. We are, in fact, imitating the heavenly pattern here in hopes of carrying these blessings into eternity. It does seem logical that if we have made family life a terrible experience for us here, the Gods will not "curse us" with families in the hereafter. On the other hand, if we can become effective husbands and wives, fathers and mothers here, what a great blessing it would be to continue such works into eternity!

Another aspect of theology has to do with our retaining the Spirit as a couple. The Holy Ghost is very sensitive to the unity and oneness of marrieds. Remember the classic story of Joseph Smith and Emma as told by David Whitmer.

> One morning when he was getting ready to continue the translation [of the Book of Mormon], something went wrong about the house and he was put out about it. Something that Emma, his wife, had done. Oliver and I went upstairs and Joseph came up soon after to continue the translation but he could not do anything. He could not translate a single syllable. He went downstairs, out into the orchard, and made supplication to the Lord; was gone about an hour—came back to the house, and asked Emma's forgiveness and then came upstairs where we were and then the translation went on all right. He could do nothing save he was humble and faithful. (B. H. Roberts, *A Comprehensive History of the Church*, 1:131.)

If Joseph Smith was "penalized" by a withdrawal of the Spirit of the Lord for offending his wife, we also must be careful in our relationship with our spouse and children. When a husband and wife argue or are negative and critical with each other, the Holy Ghost withdraws. This loss of the Spirit should impress us with the need to repent, to apologize, and to make the relationship right again. In offending our spouse we have offended the very one with whom we have made enduring commitments, and we should be anxious to invite the Spirit back.

Some marriage partners are of the opinion that they are from the "true family"; that is, they do everything right, and it is the partner that needs help. Such an attitude prevents apologies and repentance from taking place. We all need to seek the forgiveness of a spouse and children on occasion, for we all make mistakes in carrying out our family responsibilities. When one spouse apologizes to the other, a reconciliation is effected and feelings of love return as the rift is repaired and the Spirit of the Lord returns. (Repentance, of course, must be genuine, not simply a device to get the other "off your back." It assumes a commitment to not allow the same offense to be repeated.)

I mentioned earlier the need to incorporate Christlike traits into our character. Where will we have the most opportunity to acquire and practice these traits of patience, meekness, forgiveness, and so forth? Of course, it is in the home. Children have a way of testing us in these traits. Two-year-olds, for example, will test you in mercy, patience, long-suffering, charity. Teenagers will test you in mercy, patience, long-suffering, charity, gasoline consumption, money management.

Of course, we can abuse our children, we can be harsh with them, and the Lord will not strike us dead. But if we have the proper perspective, we can learn from our children the very attributes, the very character traits, that can exalt us. The task of parenting can have, as a by-product, the sanctification of the parents. Elder Boyd K. Packer has stated: "Much of what I know—of what it matters that one knows—I have learned from my children" ("Children Are an Heritage of the Lord," *Improvement Era*, Dec. 1966, p. 1150).

It is interesting to me that older couples, whose children are grown and have left home, seem to remember those events in the lives of their children which were very exasperating at the time they occurred. Now they view them with fondness and almost a pride that their children were so "creative" and "clever." Truly, crisis plus time equals humor.

I remember a man explaining his system that helps him keep the proper perspective with his children. When he comes home from work, he pretends that his children— ages fourteen, twelve, ten, nine, six, five, and two—have all grown up and left home to build families of their own. Only he and his wife still live at home. He then pretends he pleads with the Lord that he might have all his children back again as they were when they were young, for just one last night together. The Lord relents, finally, saying, "Oh, all right, but only for one night. Tomorrow they must go back to their own families!'' When he enters the door, what do you predict will happen between this father and his children?

Emotionally Stable Children

When parents have a strong marriage, the children will likely be emotionally healthy. Child psychologists declare that, above all else, every child needs the kind of loving care that comes from caring parents. Without that children become insecure and tend towards low self-esteem. Then problems surface—alienation from parents, character disorders, and often rebellion against parental values. President Harold B. Lee wrote: ''The most important thing a father can do for his children is to love their mother. And I would add to that, A woman happy with her husband is better for her children than a hundred books on child care.'' (''Be Loyal to the Royal Within You,'' *BYU Speeches of the Year* [Provo: Brigham Young University Press, 1973], p. 92.)

When a mother is upset, irritated, and frustrated with her husband, how can she soothe, calm, and teach her children in positive ways—this child who is developing a sense of independence and experiencing typical growing pains? More than likely she will respond with hostility and impatience toward her child. If children do not sense her love (and they are very sensitive to it), they may question their value and worth. They then test the love of their mother, and they have a repertoire of behavior to attract her attention, for children usually equate attention from Mom with love. If she responds to the child's attempt to attract her attention through his obnoxious, antisocial behavior, the child is rewarded for such ''acting out.''

On the other hand, when parents reciprocate love and affection, the children tend to be more secure and stable. They can treat others with kindness and feel confident about their own masculinity or femininity. It is a truism that when parents love each other, there is a greater chance that boys and girls will develop in normal, healthy ways. An eminent psychiatrist, Dr. Harold M. Voth, has written:

> The correct development of a child requires the commitment of mature parents who understand either consciously or intuitively that children do not grow up like Topsy. Good mothering from birth on provides the psychological core upon which all subsequent development takes place. Mothering is probably the most important function on earth. This is a full-time, demanding task. It requires a high order of gentleness, commitment, steadiness, capacity to give, and many other qualities, too. A woman needs a good man by her side so she will not be distracted and depleted, thus making it possible for her to provide rich humanness to her babies and children. Her needs must be met by the [husband]. Above all, she must be made secure. A good man brings out the best in a woman, who can then do her best for the children. Similarly, a good woman brings out the best in a man, who can then do his best for his wife and children. Children bring out the best in their parents. All together they make a family, a place where people of great strength are shaped, who in turn make strong societies. Our nation was built by such people. ("The Family and the Future of America." Reprinted from the *Alabama Journal of Medical Sciences*, vol. 15, no. 3 [July 1978], p. 310.)

Both boys and girls need good models of maleness and femaleness in order to develop their own sex role identification and to appreciate those of the opposite sex. Individuals from strong families tend to have a sense of personal identity. No doubt some of the homosexual behavior of the day is a product of poor sex role models.

Sexual Fulfillment

Today's media depicts the message that physical relationships—hugging, kissing, embracing, and sexual intimacy—are the ways to solve personal problems that arise between two people "in love." Such, however, is not the case. Married couples can attest that the sexual dimension of marriage is a barometer of the quality of the marriage, and is an expression of the love (or lack of love) that exists between the two. A counselor has written:

> The foundation of [sexual] relationships is good relations between husband and wife *in all other areas.* It is difficult for a wife to give of herself spontaneously and freely if she is resentful and angry with her husband. Both must work to be respectful, courteous, loving with each other in all areas of their interaction so that they can give freely and without fear of being hurt in this most intimate of relationships. . . . Both man and wife should be sensitive to those things that impede good sexual relationships. Unproductive and unresolved conflict; lack of privacy; fear of being ridiculed, hurt, dominated, or used; fear of losing oneself to another; fatigue, in-law problems; business difficulties; and lack of confidence in oneself or one's mate are among those things that most often hinder good sexual relations. (G. Hugh Allred, *How to Strengthen Your Marriage and Family* [Provo: Brigham Young University Press, 1976], p. 255.)

If sexual intimacy is to be therapeutic, both husband and wife must love and respect each other. Sexual intimacy, to be satisfying, must be preceded by a loving relationship that includes sharing personal feelings which reassure emotional commitment and closeness. Otherwise, the sexual expression in marriage is simply selfish indulgence, personal gratification, or the exploitation of the spouse for one's own use.

Lack of Good Alternatives

If a strong marriage does not exist, what are the alternatives? Neither divorce, separation, stress, tension, nor conflict is a growth option. That is not to say that we won't learn from such experiences, but that they may not lead us in the direction of eternal life. Intimacy suffers, our children will struggle with their own personal development, we may be in danger of breaking sacred covenants, our companionship is stunted, and our personal happiness flees. Perhaps that is why Church leaders have counseled us to repent, to rebuild our love for each other, end our bickering, rekindle romance, review gospel fundamentals, reacquire a testimony of the gospel plan, and apply the principles of love, charity, and forgiveness with each other. Love *can* be renewed. But often we are unwilling to pay the price of repentance and change.

Unfortunately, people who divorce to avoid further physical and verbal abuse, desertion, or wickedness of a spouse are often treated rather shabbily by the rest of us. Perhaps this stems from the fact that we stress so strongly the value of enduring family relations that when an individual "fails" in marriage, we may withdraw our support and the divorced person feels rejected. We usually do not know the circumstances surrounding a divorce; and it is none of our business, anyway. Our sole responsibility is simply to assist those who have suffered reverses in any way through the trauma that accompanies divorce.

I have talked with many divorced people in the Church who resent being treated as second-class citizens. Despite my conclusion that members do not intend to hurt others on purpose, that is nevertheless the end result. Consequently, many of these single people struggle in their activity in the Church because they feel the withdrawal of the hand of friendship and fellowship—exactly when they need it most. These brothers and sisters simply want, and deserve, to be treated as individuals, as human beings. We need to be supportive rather than judgmental. If the truth were known in many instances, it took great courage for some to seek a divorce rather than suffer in silence from abuse, negligence, irresponsible behavior, or infidelity on the part of their spouse. We can assist them in several ways—babysitting, taking their children with us for a family outing and letting the single parent have some time alone, helping with home maintenance, and being a helpful neighbor. These members need an arm of love around them rather than the stinging criticism they often receive.

Divorced persons often become bitter and angry over such treatment and grow weak in their testimony or in their resolve to remain active. They are often frustrated by constant references to family relations in church meetings.

President Spencer W. Kimball, sensitive to this problem, counseled the sisters:

> Now, the General Authorities are very much aware of the fact that many of our sisters are widows. Others have become divorced. Still others have never had the privilege of temple marriage. We want all such sisters to understand that when we speak of family life, it is not done to make them feel sad or unappreciated. . . .
>
> We have no choice, dear sisters, but to continue to hold up the ideal of the Latter-day Saint family. The fact that some do not now have the privilege of living in such a family is not reason enough to stop talking about it. We do discuss family life with sensitivity, however, realizing that many sisters do not presently have the privilege of belonging or contributing to such a family. But we cannot set aside this standard, because so many other things depend on it. . . .
>
> There is a great and grand principle involved here. Just as those who do not hear the gospel in this life, but who would have received it with all their hearts had they heard it, will be given the fulness of the gospel blessings in the next world— so, too, the women of the Church who do not in this life have the privileges and blessings of a temple marriage, through no fault of their own, who would have responded if they had an appropriate opportunity—will receive all those blessings in the world to come. We desire all you sisters to know how much we love and appreciate you. We respect you for your valiant and devoted service, and have many opportunities to observe how dedicated you are! (*Ensign*, Nov. 1978, p. 103.)

Why spend this life being miserable when we are capable of a successful and exciting marriage? We simply must have a good marriage if we are to extend these opportunities beyond this life. Can we imagine celestial beings being sarcastic to each other? punishing? involved in power struggles? temperamental? angry? revengeful? unhappy? Do we think that they play "games" to hurt? It is unthinkable. Then we too must learn to be as they are. It is essential that we make whatever efforts it takes to bring our personality and temperament into line with gospel principles if we expect these eternal possibilities.

Table 3.1

MARRIAGE EVALUATION

(Give as many answers as you can—three is only a guideline for
you to consider.)

1. How do you let your spouse know that you love him/her?
    1.
    2.
    3.

2. How does your spouse let you know that he/she loves you?
    1.
    2.
    3.

3. How would you like your spouse to show love to you?
    1.
    2.
    3.

4. What things do you appreciate most about your spouse?
    1.
    2.
    3.

5. If you could change one thing about your partner—what
   would it be?
    1.
    2.
    3.

6. List three areas you and your partner can talk about with
   ease.
    1.
    2.
    3.

7. List three areas that you and your mate find difficult to talk
   about.
    1.
    2.
    3.

8. What would you say are major problem areas in your marriage?
   1.
   2.
   3.

9. What are the major strengths in your marriage?
   1.
   2.
   3.

10. How would you rate your marriage? Circle one number from 1 to 10.

1	2	3	4	5	6	7	8	9	10
Unhappy		More downs than ups			We are healthy		We are very happy as a couple		

If your marriage is out of whack, President Spencer W. Kimball has suggested that there is hope:

> There are many people who do not find divorce attorneys and who do not end their marriages, but who have permitted their marriages to grow stale and cheap. There are spouses who have fallen from the throne of adoration and worship and are in the low state of mere joint occupancy of the home, joint sitters at the table, joint possessors of certain things that cannot be easily divided. These people are on the path that leads to trouble. These people will do well (1) to re-evaluate, (2) to renew their courting, (3) to express their affection, (4) to acknowledge kindnesses, and (5) to increase their consideration so their marriage can again become beautiful, sweet, and growing.
>
> Love is like a flower, and, like the body, it needs constant feeding. The mortal body would soon be emaciated and die if there were not frequent feedings. The tender flower would wither and die without food and water. And so love, also, cannot be expected to last forever unless it is continually fed with portions of love, the manifestation of esteem and

admiration, the expressions of gratitude, and the consideration of unselfishness. (*Marriage,* pp. 44–45; enumerations added.)

Success in family relations is based on (1) personal righteousness and (2) the quality of our family relations. Using gospel and Church standards, check your own level of Church commitment and take time, as a couple, to review table 3.1, "Marriage Evaluation." Share and discuss your responses with each other.

Priesthood and Family 4

Since The Church of Jesus Christ of Latter-day Saints is the only church which teaches that the family unit organized in mortality may become an eternal kingdom, it is important to understand how Joseph Smith received the principles and the priesthood authority to so organize families.

The restoration of the gospel and priesthood was set in motion by angels who appeared to him following the visit of the Father and the Son.

Angels	Date of Appearance	Restored
Moroni	22 September 1827	Book of Mormon plates
John the Baptist	15 May 1829	Aaronic Priesthood
Peter, James, and John	June 1829 (exact date unknown)	Melchizedek Priesthood
Moses	3 April 1836	Keys to gather Israel
Elias	3 April 1836	Blessings of Abraham
Elijah	3 April 1836	Keys of sealing

Although other angels came to the earth to instruct the young Prophet (D&C 128:20–21), the angels I have listed here restored the fulness of the gospel and specific priesthood keys that are essential to our salvation. Moroni, for example, restored the Book of Mormon plates, which provide another testament of Jesus Christ as our Savior and contain a clear account of the gospel as taught among the Nephites. This record is a great key to unlock much that is obscure and difficult in the Bible. The other angels restored priesthood power and keys needed to organize the Church, preach the gospel, gather Israel, organize an eternal family, and return the sealing powers by which all priesthood ordinances are valid.

Orders of the Priesthood

It may be helpful to look briefly at what Joseph Smith referred to as "orders of the priesthood." He explained that "all priesthood is Melchizedek, but there are different portions or degrees of it" (*Teachings of the Prophet Joseph Smith*, p. 180). He also commented that "there are three grand orders of priesthood" (ibid., p. 322). Here is a brief look at these orders.

1. *The Aaronic Priesthood.* This order of priesthood consists of four ordained offices—deacon, teacher, priest, and bishop. The bishop, who is a high priest, serves as the president of this priesthood in the ward and administers in temporal affairs. He presides over and assists each of the young men and women under his charge to prepare themselves for missions and marriage, and to learn the value of service to others.

2. *The Melchizedek Priesthood.* This order of priesthood consists of five ordained offices—elder, seventy, high priest, patriarch, and Apostle. The senior Apostle is called by the Lord to serve as the President of the Church and the President of the High Priesthood (D&C 81:2; 107:76). A bishop is also ordained a high priest to give him presiding

and administrative authority in spiritual matters within the ward.

3. *The Patriarchal Order of Priesthood.* Another "grand order" of the priesthood is called the "patriarchal order" or the "new and everlasting covenant of marriage" (D&C 131:2). Elder Bruce R. McConkie has said of this order: "[a couple] can enter an order of the priesthood named the new and everlasting covenant of marriage (See D&C 131:2), named also the patriarchal order, because of which order we can create for ourselves eternal family units of our own, patterned after the family of God our Heavenly Father." ("Priesthood Activation," *Ensign*, May 1982 p. 34.)

This order of priesthood is associated with a temple marriage. The initial "offices" or callings of this order are those of husband and wife. A couple is "sealed" together in an eternal covenant by priesthood authority. They receive the authority to use their procreative powers to bear children—thereby assisting the Lord in his great work of exaltation for his spirit children (D&C 132:63). The authorized use of these sexual powers, of course, is limited to legally married couples. President Spencer W. Kimball counseled, "There should be total chastity of men and women before marriage and total fidelity in marriage" (*The Teachings of Spencer W. Kimball* [Salt Lake City: Bookcraft, 1982], p. 264).

With the birth of children (or through adoption), the titles of father and mother are activated. It is noteworthy that these callings—husband-father, wife-mother—are the most important "offices" held by individuals either in mortal life or in eternity. In our prayers we do not call upon the "High Priest of the universe." We probably petition God as our Heavenly Father. Elder H. Burke Peterson stated: "In this life a father is never released from his responsibility. We call bishops, and they serve for a time and are released. Stake presidents likewise are called, serve, and are released. *But a father's calling is an eternal*

calling if he lives worthily.'' (''The Father's Duty to Foster
the Welfare of His Family,'' *Ensign,* Nov. 1977 p. 87;
emphasis added.) The same holds true for mothers.

In discussing the candidates for exaltation, the Lord
indicated that ''they are they who are priests and kings,
who have received of his fulness, and of his glory'' (D&C
76:56). Elder Bruce R. McConkie explained: ''Those who
endure in perfect faith, who receive the Melchizedek
Priesthood, and who gain the blessings of the temple
(including celestial marriage) are eventually ordained *kings*
and *priests*. These are offices given faithful holders of the
Melchizedek Priesthood, and in them they will bear rule as
exalted beings during the millennium and in eternity.''
(*Mormon Doctrine,* 2nd ed. [Salt Lake City: Bookcraft,
1966], p. 599.) He further stated:

> If righteous men have power through the gospel and its
> crowning ordinance of celestial marriage to become kings
> and priests to rule in exaltation forever, it follows that the
> women by their side (without whom they cannot attain exal-
> tation) will be *queens* and priestesses. (Rev. 1:6; 5:10.) Exalta-
> tion grows out of the eternal union of a man and his wife. Of
> those whose marriage endures in eternity, the Lord says,
> ''Then shall *they* be gods'' (D&C 132:20); that is, each of
> them, the man and the woman, will be a god. As such they
> will rule over their dominions forever. (Ibid., p. 613.)

While the offices of king and queen signify potentiali-
ties for us, in that they relate not to mortals but to resurrected and exalted beings, for purposes of comparison we
may perhaps apply them in a general way to the little kingdom of the family. In marriage, the ''subjects'' of this
newly formed kingdom are the children born (or adopted)
in the new and everlasting covenant of marriage. As
''rulers,'' parents are to teach each ''citizen'' under their
jurisdiction how to live and function within the earthly
kingdom of home, city, and country. The ''subjects'' are to
be instructed with regard to property, human relations,
rules of conduct, and the observance of all the laws that are
essential in maintaining order in an earthly (and later,

heavenly) kingdom. (Have you noticed that if you don't rule in your kingdom, the subjects will?)

Married couples are commissioned to oversee the physical, social, emotional, intellectual, and spiritual growth of their offspring. Even as Jesus "increased in wisdom and stature, and in favour with God and man" (Luke 2:52), so parents have the responsibility to assist their children in these phases of their development.

These sacred callings are, of course, conditional at the time of marriage. A temple marriage confers certain blessings and promises, but it does not grant exaltation. Only a faithful observance of all the laws and covenants associated with the marriage can do that. (However, by the "holy spirit of promise," every member of the Church may receive divine assurance, in mortality, that all earthly ordinances in which they participated will extend into eternity for them. See Joseph Fielding Smith, *Doctrines of Salvation*, 2:94–95.)

The order of marriage, or patriarchal order, provides a husband and wife with the privilege of continuing in eternity that which they begin in this life. (See D&C 131:1–4; 132:30.) These priesthood orders are of such importance that we need to understand how they were restored. The following text portrays the three "grand orders" of the priesthood as they were restored in chronological sequence. All priesthood is Melchizedek, as the Prophet Joseph Smith taught, and comes under the direction of the First Presidency. The Patriarchal order will be more fully operative during the millennium and eternity. We enter this order in a temple marriage as a couple.

Restoration of Priesthood

The Aaronic Priesthood was restored by John the Baptist to Joseph Smith and Oliver Cowdery on May 15, 1829. Within a month or so of this experience, Peter, James, and John, Apostles of the Lord in the meridian of time, restored the Melchizedek Priesthood. Elder Bruce R.

McConkie has written: "The Melchizedek Priesthood is the highest and holiest order ever given to men on earth. It is the power and authority to do all that is necessary to save and exalt the children of men. It is the very priesthood held by the Lord Jesus Christ himself and by virtue of which he was able to gain eternal life in the kingdom of his Father." ("Priesthood Activation," *Ensign*, May 1982, p. 33.)

These two priesthoods, or more accurately, two divisions of the Melchizedek Priesthood (D&C 107:5), were restored in 1829. The Church was subsequently organized in April of 1830. The First Presidency, Quorum of the Twelve Apostles, high councils, and Church Patriarch came later. However, in the year 1836 an important event occurred wherein the Savior, Moses, Elias, and Elijah appeared to Joseph Smith and Oliver Cowdery in the Kirtland Temple and restored specific keys of the Melchizedek Priesthood.

Moses. Moses restored a specialized key of missionary work to search the earth for the house of Israel and to lead the lost tribes back to Zion (D&C 110:11). In 1837 Church missionaries were called to the first overseas proselyting assignments—in England. Today we are nearing two hundred missions encircling the globe. We need our young men, many sisters, and large numbers of couples to be willing and able to go into the far reaches of the world to share the message of the Restoration and gather Israel. The prophets have promised that if we sufficiently increase the number of missionaries, the Lord will provide a way for them to enter the nations of the earth that now do not permit this. For this to happen, however, parents must teach their children of their responsibility to serve missions both at home and abroad.

Elias. "After this [Moses' visit], Elias appeared, and committed the dispensation of the gospel of Abraham, saying that in us and our seed all generations after us should be blessed" (D&C 110:12). These blessings include the gospel and the priesthood, and the responsibility to administer them to all nations. From this revelation we learn that Elias restored the blessings associated with the priesthood "order of marriage." (See D&C 131:1-4.) Recall that Abraham's seed were given the promise and privilege to take the gospel to the world (Abraham 2:9-11). Now, once again, in our day children born in the covenant are heirs to all the blessings of the great patriarch. These children have the "right" to serve as missionaries, to marry in the temple, and to obtain the fulness of the gospel in their own quest for eternal life. It is their right and privilege to receive these blessings because they were born to parents who received the promises of that covenant when they married in the temple. The children are heirs to a fulness of the gospel and the priesthood. Such blessings include the promise of eternal increase. (See D&C 132:29-32.)

One further point. Couples who marry in the temple have the promise that the spirits assigned to them as their mortal offspring were among the faithful and valiant of the Father's spirit children in the premortal world. Elder Bruce R. McConkie wrote: "Alma taught the great truth that every person who holds the Melchizedek Priesthood was foreordained to receive that high and holy order in the pre-existent councils of eternity" (*Mormon Doctrine*, p. 290).

As the children of couples married in the temple are born in the covenant, they are automatically eligible for the fulness of the gospel and priesthood, and therefore, according to Alma's teaching, must have been foreordained to receive this blessing before they came to the earth (Alma 13:3-5). That promise is part of what Elias restored.[1] Elder McConkie explained:

---

1. Couples who are sealed after they were first married civilly are given the promise that any children born to them before the temple sealing will receive at the time of their sealing to the parents the same blessings as if the children had initially been born to the parents in the new and everlasting covenant of marriage. This suggests that the Lord, knowing ahead of time who will come into the Church, or who will become active, assigns spirit children so that no blessing will be lost to the parents because of circumstances beyond their control, such as not even knowing the Church or priesthood existed.

Now what was the gospel of Abraham [restored by Elias]? Obviously it was the commission, the mission, the endowment and power, the message of salvation, given to Abraham. . . . It was a divine promise that both in the world and out of the world his seed should continue "as innumerable as the stars; or, if ye were to count the sand upon the seashore ye could not number them. . . ."

Thus the gospel of Abraham was one of celestial marriage; . . . *it was a gospel or commission to provide a lineage for the elect portion of the pre-existent spirits.* . . . This power and commission is what Elias restored. (*Mormon Doctrine*, pp. 219–220; emphasis added.)

The commission to "provide a lineage" refers to the authority to bear children that is conferred upon a couple at marriage. Then the Lord honors them with a faithful spirit from the premortal life. This opportunity to bring valiant spirit children of the Father to the earth is part of our commitment to be responsible parents. We are rearing Heavenly Father's children in his behalf.

The temple is the only place on the earth where these promises are conferred. How blessed we are as Latter-day Saints to be the recipients of these blessings restored by Elias and to have the privilege of having temples available to us! The Lord explained:

In the celestial glory there are three heavens or degrees;

And in order to obtain the highest [degree], a man *must* enter into this *order of the priesthood* [meaning the new and everlasting covenant of marriage];

And if he does not [enter that order of marriage], he cannot obtain it [meaning the highest degree—exaltation].

He may enter into the other, but that is the end of his kingdom; he cannot have an increase [posterity]. (D&C 131:1–4; emphasis added.)

Elijah. To illustrate the keys restored by Elijah, suppose that a couple, in preparing for an eternal marriage ceremony, goes to one of their bishops and asks, "Bishop, will you come to the temple and perform our marriage for us?" The bishop, of course, must decline. So they go to a stake president and make a similar request. They will receive the same answer from him. Why? Because even the stake president, although he is a high priest and presides over a large number of Saints, does not by virtue of that calling hold the sealing power restored by Elijah. This priesthood authority, which operates under the direction of the First Presidency, is conferred only on the General Authorities, temple presidencies, and men called and set apart as sealers in each temple to assist in the ordinance work therein. Therefore, unless the two marry in the temple where this sealing power is available, they cannot benefit from the priesthood keys restored by Elijah.

Elijah confirmed to the Prophet Joseph Smith that with his coming all essential priesthood keys to prepare the Saints for the coming of the Savior had been restored: "Therefore, the keys of this dispensation are committed into your hands; and by this ye may know that the great and dreadful day of the Lord is near, even at the doors" (D&C 110:16).

Because of the sacred nature and eternal significance of the fulness of the gospel and of the priesthood in the over-all plan of the Lord to exalt families, they are conferred only in the most holy of settings—a temple. The most important reason for a couple to marry in the temple, then, is that these blessings can be received only there. Of those who fail to obtain these blessings, the Lord declared: "For these angels did not abide my law (of marriage); therefore, they cannot be enlarged, but remain separately and singly, without exaltation, . . . to all eternity; and from henceforth are not gods, but are angels of God forever and ever." (D&C 132:17.)

Can we imagine the possibility of not continuing family associations beyond this life—ever again? Can we fathom the implications of not having further posterity or maybe not even access to those who have been our mortal family —because of our carelessness with regard to priesthood ordinances and covenants?

Consider the implications of the foregoing on various aspects of marriage and family relations.

1. *Dating.* It is very important to teach and monitor our

children in their dating years. No wonder President Spencer W. Kimball counseled that there be no dating until age sixteen. Even then we are to date very carefully, and only with people with similar values, an eternal perspective, and a commitment to the gospel. ("The Marriage Decision," *Ensign*, 1975, p. 4.) Marriage is the most important mortal decision we make, and it has far-reaching and eternal implications. This decision requires a wide range of dating partners, time and maturity, careful thought and study, and the inspiration and confirmation of the Spirit of the Lord. Parents must exercise a firm but loving hand during these years when children think they are more prepared for heterosexual interaction than they really are. If we stay close to them, and establish warm relationships with our teenagers, we *can* influence them to date and court wisely. Rules about hours, places, frequency of dating, manners, deportment, and the quality of dating partners are topics that parents will want to discuss with their children.

2. *Moral cleanliness.* The Lord limits sexual intimacy to marriage. Children need instruction on moral issues and sex education from loving parents—more so than from extra-familial organizations which do not have the same interest or doctrinal foundations. Children should know that self-control and self-discipline must supersede selfishness, particularly in this area of handling the very powers of God.

We understand that we have all of eternity in which to procreate children if we will rightly use these powers and keep all other commandments of God in this life. It is good and right to experience sexual intimacy, but only within the bounds the Lord has set. True love is founded squarely on the foundation of chastity. Our social order is currently mired in a less lofty perspective of male and female relations. Our children must be able to detect the sophistry and cunning of the devil, who is the father of lies and whose desire and ambition is to destroy men and women by corrupting the very fountain of life. Parents are responsible to teach morality and chastity clearly.

3. *Strong marriages.* Our greatest investment in time and effort should be to safeguard and build strong, happy marriages. Without the foundation of such marriages our social fabric will disintegrate very rapidly. Signs of such decay have already reached the ominous level. The world is quickly losing the vision of what marriage can accomplish. Latter-day Saints must demonstrate to the world not only that marriage is the Lord's way but also that we can have great happiness and success as couples in rearing healthy and happy children. It requires our very best effort to succeed in marriage. We must continue to court each other and monitor our marriage commitment and partnership following the ceremony. A temple marriage carries great promises, but is no guarantee of eternal life. President Marion G. Romney explained:

> These fruits of the gospel—assurance that we shall obtain eternal life, peace in this world sustained by such an assurance, and finally eternal life in the world to come—are within the reach of us all. Sometimes, however, because of our lack of understanding and appreciation of them, I am persuaded that we take too much for granted. We assume that because we are members of the Church, we shall receive as a matter of course all the blessings of the gospel. I have heard people contend that they have a claim upon them because they have been through the temple, even though they are not careful to keep the covenants they there made. I do not think this will be the case.
>
> We might take a lesson from an account given by the Prophet of a vision of the resurrection, *in which he records that one of the saddest things he had ever witnessed was the sorrow of members of the Church who came forth to a resurrection below that which they had taken for granted they would receive.* ("Fruits of the Gospel," *Improvement Era,* Nov. 1949, pp. 752, 754; emphasis added.)

Our Heavenly Father has restored to the earth in our day the essential ordinances, covenants, and gospel principles for us to gain eternal life, but it is up to each one of us to seek them and obtain them.

4. *Desire to have children.* Is it clear why we as Latter-day Saints are pro-family? pro-children? anti-abortion? If the Lord is sending spirits to the earth who have been reserved and foreordained to carry out his great work in this present dispensation, it is our privilege to bear and rear them and to help them catch the vision of their destiny.

> Our young people are among the most blessed and favored of our Father's children. They are the nobility of heaven, a choice and chosen generation who have a divine destiny. Their spirits have been reserved to come forth in this day when the gospel is on the earth, and when the Lord needs valiant servants to carry on His great latter-day work. (President Joseph Fielding Smith, in Conference Report, Apr. 1970, p. 6.)

In what better way could Satan thwart the work of God than in convincing people that there is no need to bear children? that they are too expensive to raise? that women need careers not motherhood in order to feel fulfilled? Voices cry out that mothering is obsolete, that to postpone or prevent the birth of children is the mark of sophistication and culture, that children are no longer valuable or needed in an urban setting.

In contrast, what a privilege to be the parents of some of the finest spirits to come to this earth!

> To carry forward his own purposes among men and nations, the Lord foreordained chosen spirit children in pre-existence and assigned them to come to earth at particular times and places. . . . These pre-existence appointments . . . simply designated certain individuals to perform missions which the Lord in his wisdom knew they had the talents and capacities to do.
>
> The mightiest and greatest spirits were foreordained to stand as prophets and spiritual leaders. . . . In all this there is not the slightest hint of compulsion; persons foreordained to fill special missions in mortality are as abundantly endowed with free agency as are any other persons. By their

foreordination the Lord merely gives them the opportunity to serve him and his purposes if they will choose to measure up to the standards he knows they are capable of attaining. (Bruce R. McConkie, *Mormon Doctrine,* 2nd edition [Salt Lake City: Bookcraft, 1966], p. 290.)

5. *Effective parenting practices.* Although these valiant spirits were reserved to be sent to the earth now, they have come at a time of great challenge. President Harold B. Lee warned:

> But now there is a warning: Despite that calling which is spoken of in the scriptures as "foreordination," we have another inspired declaration: "Behold, there are many called, but few are chosen. . . ." (D&C 121:34.)
>
> This suggests that even though we have our free agency here, there are many who were foreordained before the world was, to a greater state than they have prepared themselves for here. Even though they might have been among the noble and great, from among whom the Father declared he would make his chosen leaders, they may fail of that calling here in mortality. Then the Lord poses this question: ". . . and why are they not chosen?" (D&C 121:34.)
>
> Two answers were given—First, "Because their hearts are set so much upon the things of this world. . . ." And second, they ". . . aspire to the honors of men." (D&C 121:35.) (*Ensign,* Jan. 1974, p. 5.)

As parents, we must make sure that our children carry out their foreordinations in these last days. The Lord is sending his children into our homes with the challenge that we prepare them for their latter-day work. This task requires great effort, for it is a day of wickedness and we have been warned that even some of the "elect according to the covenant," shall falter. (Joseph Smith—Matthew 1:22.) We must parent well.

No wonder the prophets have asked us to gather our families together for prayer and for family home evenings to teach them of their divine mission—to establish Zion. How will they ever come to see why they should go on missions or be married in the temple if we don't give them some good reasons and be good models ourselves? This dispensation needs great homes where fathers and mothers will teach the gospel with clarity and power so that the rising generation is prepared to move the cause of Zion forward. It is in the homes that the battle will be won or lost.

Wilford Woodruff said:

> There never was a dispensation on the earth when prophets and apostles, the inspiration, revelation and power of God, the holy priesthood and the keys of the kingdom were needed more than they are in this generation. There never has been a dispensation when the friends of God and righteousness among the children of men needed more faith in the promises and prophecies than they do to-day; and there certainly never has been a generation of people on the earth that has had a greater work to perform than the inhabitants of the earth in the latter days. (*Journal of Discourses*, 15:8.)

Practices   II

Common Problems   5

In the spring and summer months we spend a considerable amount of time attending wedding receptions—beautiful, extravagant affairs where families join together to show off their children and extend their support and love to the marrying couple. The "in-laws" greet and size up the "out-laws" and everyone seems in a festive mood. We are sure that this couple made a wise choice in selecting each other from the myriads of possibilities. We have confidence that following the reception they will sail off happily into the sunset. Have you ever been to an unhappy reception?

When we begin marriage, we are full of hope, excitement, and love. We are sure that none of the problems others have encountered will happen to us. But somehow they do. And usually we are at a loss to know why. We are decent people. We want to succeed. We've been active in the Church. We love the Lord and our spouse, but somehow the anticipation of marriage and family living is not quite the same as the reality of it. And accepting less than what we hope for is not easy.

What begins as a wonderful path to glory often becomes sadly sidetracked. Brent and Nichole had a whirlwind courtship. They married when he was thirty and she was twenty-four. Brent had worked for years and had saved enough money to pay cash for their first little home. They looked forward to their life together. Knowing that he was out of school and a good wage earner, Nichole set about to enjoy her affluence. She furnished every room in the house. She papered, painted, remodeled, put new siding on the outside of the home, and charged everything. Brent, cautious with his money (how else would he have saved enough to pay cash for a house?) was upset, but didn't want to complain, and couldn't bring himself to discuss the issue with Nichole. Instead, after work each evening he retired to the back yard where he created an incredible flower and vegetable garden. He didn't stop in the kitchen because there was never any dinner prepared there. Nichole didn't know much about cooking. She spent her days decorating her house and talking to her many friends on the phone. She was especially thrilled when she found out she was going to have a baby. Spontaneous, impetuous, carefree, generous, and fun-loving, she had always loved children and looked forward to motherhood.

Brent continued working the garden, and soon the kitchen counters were covered with his beautiful fruits and vegetables. He took great pride in his yard and his produce. The trouble was, since Nichole didn't cook, the produce rotted on the counter. She was not interested in canning or homemaking. She wanted Brent to spend more time with her. They never went places and had few friends as a couple. She begged him to take her out for an evening; he piled more vegetables on the kitchen countertop. Toward the end of her pregnancy, mired in vegetables and mounds of unwashed laundry, she accidentally discovered that Brent was seeing another woman. She was devastated and sought counseling and wanted to start over. He didn't care to talk about it.

Brent and Nichole started out as good people. Their parents were proud of them. Their neighbors loved them and everyone thought they had a great marriage. They each had positive character traits. They were active in the Church. But they also ignored problems that developed, until they could no longer handle them. They failed to deal with reality and did not check in with each other to monitor their progress as a married couple.

There are a number of pitfalls—traps, really—that even good people can fall into. Let's look at some of them.

1. *Selfishness.* By this I mean an inability to see a situation from any other point of view than our own. Of course we all think we are right, that our perception of reality is accurate. We wouldn't have opinions if we hadn't thought them through and decided they were correct. So, how can another "good person" that we happen to marry have a different outlook on the same matter?

President Kimball identified selfishness as the basic element in relationship disorders, while communication, sex, money, in-laws, and similar concerns are merely outward symptoms of the more fundamental problem of self-centeredness. (*Marriage*, p. 19.) One of the hardest things we ever do in a marriage (or elsewhere) is to set aside our own feelings for a few minutes and listen to the feelings and thoughts of our spouse. I don't mean a mere superficial listening—the kind where we can hardly wait for them to finish so we can say what's on our mind—but a genuine interest.

"I raised this garden for you, and you couldn't care less!" yelled Brent.

"And I decorated this house for you and *you* couldn't care less!" retorted Nichole.

"You never listen to me," "You're not interested in me," "How many times do we have to go over this?" "You're the world's worst communicator," "You're just like your mother!" Negative, emotion-laden statements, sarcastic and selfish responses which block the development of love feelings between husband and wife.

If we can let go of our expectations and our own needs for the moment, and listen, reflect, reconsider, explain, or take another look at our own behavior or point of view, then we are apt to be more successful. If Nichole could have seen that perhaps dinner on the table at six with some homegrown vegetables was really important to Brent, would bring some joy to him, and would show him that she prized his green thumb, perhaps he would have tried to be more companionable. And if Brent had relaxed his enthusiasm (escape?) for the garden a bit and spent some time being interested in Nichole and her projects and pregnancy, he could have fostered better feelings between them.

If we let them, love, respect, patience, calmness, and a clear unemotional exchange of ideas can resolve most differences. That is why the scriptures stress the condition of our hearts. It is good to improve ourselves and develop our talents and interests. We are all unique in many ways. However, when we are part of a marriage and family relationship we must be willing to sacrifice the "I want" frequently. If not, the results will be damaging. As followers of Christ, we need to monitor ourselves as to whether we are humble, teachable, patient with one another, kind, long-suffering, charitable, and willing to communicate to work through differences. When we err, we must be quick to apologize, to retrace, to rectify and restore, because we are, after all, eternal companions, assisting each other toward exaltation.

2. *An over-preoccupation with who or what is right* (the returned missionary syndrome). Sometimes we are especially concerned about what is right. Maybe it comes from the mission field orientation where we constantly bear testimony: "I know that the Church is true, that I'm right, that this principle is true, and so on." The inference is that if we are right, then the other party must be wrong. Where religious truth is involved that may be necessary and understandable. But there may be some danger in thinking that we can never err in mortality. Have you ever been in a

Sunday School class, for example, where brother "Right-Answer" thought that the class was for him and the teacher alone? Even if he is "right," others feel frustrated. A preoccupation with rightness can be irritating in a marriage.

I asked a husband to give me an example of a situation that would illustrate a problem in his marriage. He began, "Last Wednesday evening, we jumped in the car to go and pick up a couple of things, and—"

His wife interrupted him, "It wasn't Wednesday, it was Thursday."

"No, it wasn't," he replied. "I remember because we picked up some dog food and—" She interrupted again, "It was too Thursday because that is the day when I get my hair done. See," she looked at me, "he doesn't even know what day it was."

Sometimes being right in a classroom or a marriage is more important to us than listening and trying to understand the "real" message and feelings of others. When our spouse or one of the children shares something, we sometimes anticipate their response, jump in, interrupt, cut them off, complete their sentences for them, or quickly judge the merit of their ideas. We may be poor listeners and act as if our superior age, or intellect, or understanding prevents error—all of which can be exasperating.

In intimate family relations, being less dogmatic and more tentative will be helpful. Statements like "Perhaps we could try this" or "See what you think about this idea" help encourage discussion and lead towards a solution. "Do you think this is a possibility?" or "How does this sound to you?" or "Does this have any merit?" will go much further in developing family harmony.

3. *We cause the very things we gripe about.* Do you recall the Savior's reference to a man looking for a sliver in his neighbor's eye and he had the equivalent of a two-by-four sticking out of his own (Matthew 7:3). Though we don't actually cause the behavior of others, we may greatly influence it. Parents of teenagers, for example, often com-

plain that their kids are unwilling to share their ideas and feelings with the parents. Yet when I ask the parents what happens when the children have a "slumber party," they confess that the children stay up all night talking with their friends. In fact, they would rather talk than sleep. The parents will say, "But take them to the store with you and you have to play Twenty Questions to avoid profound silence. Their entire vocabulary consists of yes, no, what's for dinner? I'll be home at 5:00, and is there any gas in the car? You're lucky if you get anything out of them."

Now, is it possible that parents discourage children from sharing feelings and ideas? Yes! As adults, we like to lecture, moralize, interrupt, and criticize their ideas and requests without listening. The children feel put down when they risk with us. Communication in this instance becomes superficial. Who wants to be punished for asking or sharing? Though parents complain that their children *won't* communicate, it is the parents themselves who have trained the children to be silent. (Of course, children may learn that silence is a trump card to be played to punish or "get back." But before jumping at that excuse, take a good look at the communication patterns that exist between you and your children.)

A distraught wife once called me to say that her husband had left her and that she was beside herself with grief. I invited her in for a meeting. As we met, she was very articulate and attractive. (Visits with only one spouse tend to create the illusion that the absent party is the real culprit and the primary cause of any marital difficulties.) "Well," I finally said, "without your husband's input we aren't going to figure out why he left you. I can't see any reason why he should. Perhaps you could ask him to come with you and help us." She was not optimistic that he would, but she agreed to try. She called the next morning quite happy that he would come in for a visit with her. In a meeting with both of them it became apparent that a major portion of the problem was hers. When I asked her husband a question, she would interrupt him or answer for him and sermonize for several minutes on the subject I asked about, completely dominating the conversation.

This pattern was not obvious when just the two of us met, and it now became rather annoying to me, too. Finally, frustrated myself, I said to her, "Wait a minute! Don't you see what you're doing?" She looked puzzled, and I described to her my own reaction to her irritating, interrupting, dominating pattern. I wanted to get away from her myself. As I described my reaction to her, out of the corner of my eye, I could see her husband nodding his head in agreement with me.

After finishing my explanation to her, I turned to him and asked, "Do you ever see her doing this to you?" Emotionally, through clenched teeth, he replied, "All the time!" She was shocked at his answer, and I asked him to describe her behavior and his reaction to it. She was now teachable. As he told her of his frustration at trying to "break through" and relate to her, she was humbled and could see how she monopolized the communication, and was quite apologetic. (He had been certain that she would never allow him to be an equal partner in this marriage, and so he had simply withdrawn from the relationship.)

At work, however, he had found the receptionist to be a great listener. She encouraged him to open up and share with her. As the relationship at home deteriorated, strong feelings began to develop between these two at work. He decided he had married the wrong person and was out to make the switch.

The wife was able to change her actions and responses and the couple resolved their problem of communication. It is interesting to note, however, that her primary complaint to me about him—besides the fact that he had left her—was, "How can I get my husband to talk to me? I get so tired of talking to myself. He's over there reading the paper or watching TV." She seemed unaware that she had trained him to be quiet around her, and she thought that *he* was a poor communicator.

This is not uncommon in many relationships. Elder

Boyd K. Packer illustrated the need for each of us to take responsibility for the part we play in any problem:

> Quoting from the twenty-first verse: and as they did eat, he said, Verily I say unto you, that one of you shall betray me. (Matthew 26:21)
>
> I remind you that these men were apostles. They were of apostolic stature. It has always been interesting to me that they did not on that occasion, nudge one another and say, "I'll bet that it's old Judas. He has surely been queer lately." It reflects something of their stature. Rather it is recorded that: They were exceedingly sorrowful, and began every one of them to say unto him, Lord is it I?" ("Follow the Brethren," *Speeches of the Year* [Provo: Brigham Young University Press, 1965].)

We all must be brave enough to ask, "Lord, is it I that am causing unhappiness in my own home? Is it I who am keeping my children from opening up with me because of the way I respond to them? Is my sarcasm and critical nature the real problem?"

4. *Use of anger to manipulate or intimidate others.* Richard was a highly aggressive, highly energetic, highly motivated man. He was also easily frustrated when things did not go his way. One evening when he was returning home tired from the office, he was greeted by the confusion of his wife's last-minute dinner preparations and the rambunctiousness of four young children. As they sat down to the table (ten minutes later than he had "specified" to his wife), Lisa, the youngest child, began to fuss about dinner. Richard told her to stop and "settle down." She wailed louder. In a flash, Richard picked up her plate and hurled it across the room, dumping its contents to the floor. He threw his chair aside and stormed out of the room and house, yelling that he was going out somewhere to have his dinner in peace. The children huddled in the corner crying. Ellen, his wife, sat stunned, trembling, her stomach churning.

Anger is a great destroyer of family relations. People use it because they don't have the maturity to develop better means to handle frustration. Often it is because anger has served them effectively over the years. Richard got what he wanted—a release from his frustrations, a vent for his anger, and a quiet dinner. He thought he was justified because he had worked hard all day and "deserved" a quiet, on-time meal. But he also filled his family with fear, tension, and stress, and they, in turn, were angry at him. He had little understanding of just how intimidating his angry outbursts were to his family. He was not afraid of himself, so the extent of *their fear* just did not occur to him. He was a poor model for his children, acting at an emotional level even younger than their years. And he could not understand why he couldn't return to the family later in the evening and act as if nothing had happened. Nor could he comprehend why his wife was not eager to respond to his amorous advances.

There is simply no place for this kind of temper display in loving human relationships. It is selfishness in its highest sense. Richard could never hope to win the love and respect of his children, and his family could never hope to progress toward righteous goals with him at its head, until he learned to control his anger. He is far from the kind of leader his family needs. He needs to repent and change, to be a better teacher and model.

> Someone has said, "The size of a man may be measured by the size of the things that make him angry." How true that is! To become upset and infuriated over trivial matters gives evidence of childishness and immaturity in a person. . . .
>
> Anger against *things* is senseless indeed!
>
> Because a wrench slips and we bruise our hand is no reason for throwing the wrench halfway across a wheat field. . . .
>
> Anger against *things* is bad enough, but when it is directed against people and it flares up with white-hot fury and caustic words, we have the makings of a tragedy! . . .
>
> The man [or woman] with an uncontrolled temper is like an undisciplined child—he expresses his emotions explosively or by sulking, and disregards the feelings of those

about him. In the home, anger should be controlled and love should abound. . . .

. . . To lose our temper, to explode, to become ugly, punitive, and hateful when faced with frustrations is inexcusable! (ElRay L. Christiansen, *Ensign*, June 1971, pp. 37–38.)

5. *Unrighteous exercise of authority.* Some men confuse being the head of the family with power and control. A good friend, an ecclesiastical leader, once had a husband drag his wife in to see him so that he could counsel her that the patriarchal order called for her to be obedient and submissive to his direction. My friend, upon seeing the problem, replied to the man, "I'm sorry, but you don't even hold the priesthood." The man, a high priest, quoted his authority line in response. My friend repeated, "I'm sorry, but you don't hold the priesthood." After several protests the man calmed down. "I guess I don't know what you mean."

"Let's look it up and see what the Lord counseled." They turned together to Doctrine and Covenants 121 and read:

> That the rights of the priesthood are inseparably connected with the powers of heaven, and that the powers of heaven cannot be controlled nor handled only upon the principles of righteousness. . . . But when we undertake to cover our sins, or to gratify our pride, our vain ambition, or to exercise control or dominion or compulsion upon the souls of the children of men, in any degree of unrighteousness, behold, the heavens withdraw themselves; the Spirit of the Lord is grieved; and when it is withdrawn, Amen to the priesthood or the authority of that man.
>
> We have learned . . . that it is the nature and disposition of almost all men, as soon as they get a little authority, as they suppose, they will immediately begin to exercise unrighteous dominion.
>
> No power or influence can or ought to be maintained by virtue of the priesthood, only by persuasion, by long-

suffering, by gentleness and meekness, and by love un-feigned;

By kindness, and pure knowledge, which shall greatly enlarge the soul without hypocrisy, and without guile. (D&C 121:36–37, 39, 41–42.)

Whenever we attempt to coerce a member of our family, we breed rebellion. A parent who dominates his children is contributing to their low self-esteem and a poor self-image. Though discipline may be necessary and desirable with children, *it has no place at all with a spouse.* A wife is a partner, a companion, not one of the children.

Parents must be pleasant and patient, seeking opinions, feedback, and feelings from family members when a decision needs to be made. "This is the way I want it done!" will not do. We are to lead righteously, with charity, kindness, and a willingness to listen and compromise rather than trying to direct and control others. Persuasion is a better method.

6. *Different male and female training.* Even though there is some movement away from this, as children, boys and girls are socialized quite differently. Boys are taught to be tough, aggressive, action-oriented. Girls are taught to be quiet, reflective, well-behaved, and nurturing. Many of these qualities help prepare girls for marriage. Typical masculine character traits are not so helpful. Women marry expecting to share emotions, feelings, and ideas with their husbands. But feelings are not always easy for men to understand or express. It is frustrating for a wife to find that her husband does not deal well with feelings, and his inability to share with her may create a number of communication problems.

Of course, men have emotions and feelings, but they are discouraged at an early age from verbalizing about them. Men seldom seek catharsis—talking through a problem. They tend to keep emotions inside, bottled up. Perhaps that is why men often suffer from such stress-related illnesses as heart attacks, strokes, high blood pressure, ulcers, and colitis, and die before their wives do. (If this theory is valid, then a wife might be therapeutic to her husband by encouraging him to express his feelings and ideas freely without fear that such risking is unmanly.)

Men tend to express their emotions in physical ways. They love activity, athletics, rough-housing. They also express love feelings physically. Women are generally more adept at separating love and sex, while males generally tend to *equate them*. If a husband initiates a hug and kiss with his wife, she enjoys it and is accepting. If a wife initiates a hug and embrace with her husband, however, he may view it as a "proposition." To him love is expressed through sexual intimacy. Wives report to me, "I have stopped initiating hugging, kissing, and affection with my husband in the daytime—because I haven't got time to jump in bed in the middle of the day. The children are coming home from school; or I have clothes in the washer and things to do!" What a shame that two people cannot express love for each other without its always leading to the bedroom, or the husband's feeling rejected.

A wife may confide, "The only time my husband tells me that he loves me is when we make love." If that were the only time a husband actually expressed his feelings for his wife, she would probably wonder whether he really loves her or simply enjoys sex. A common response of women is: "I have all the sex I want; that is not my problem. What I really would like is more nonsexual attention and affection, the kind we shared before we married, when we were dating and did not share sexual intimacy." It is important to wives, especially, that their husbands show genuine affection after the ceremony, and that they convey love feelings in both sexual and nonsexual ways. Of course, the same holds true for wives.

The point of this is that sometimes we bring with us into a marriage character flaws, habits, or perspectives that make it difficult for us to be effective marriage partners or parents. It is important that as we recognize these shortcomings in ourselves, we do everything in our power to correct them.

7. *Blaming attitude.* Sometimes in marriage we lose sight of the positive dimensions of our relationship and concentrate almost exclusively on the things that are wrong. We conclude that it is our spouse's inadequacies that are causing the problems—not our own—and the evidence is easy to find. Negative patterns develop which are critical and habitual. Sustained over time, the entire marriage relationship may become colored. Some couples actually seem to enjoy "pushing buttons" to hurt each other—probably attempting to boost their own feelings of self-worth. They may even take their offenses and criticisms to outsiders in an effort to justify the way they are acting. Such actions may become so automatic that individuals are not conscious of the severe damage that results.

I remember a couple who criticized each other for some time before I intervened with the husband. Since it was a second marriage for both of them, they did not want a divorce. I asked the husband, "Well, what can *you* do to improve this marriage?" He reacted as if I had just asked him for the location of the lost tribes! He repeated hesitatingly, "What can *I* do to improve the marriage?" That had never occurred to him. All he knew was that he had brought his wife in to me to get "fixed," and he was going to wait patiently while I "rearranged some chromosomes" or did something magical. His wife had, in the previous half hour, given him at least thirty suggestions. But he did not pick one thing from her offering. His suggestion was that "before I go from work to the golf course I ought to call her and let her know where I am going." He thought that might make a major contribution to her happiness!

Assuming that the wife was better prepared for what I was asking, to take some responsibility for their plight, I asked her, "What do you think *you* can do to improve this marriage?" Stumbling over the question, she repeated, "What can I do to improve our marriage?" It seemed to be a new thought to her also. She just wanted her husband to change. We tend to look for evidence justifying ourselves as the "good guy" and our spouse as the "bad guy." But both of us must take responsibility for any problem, forsake it and the destructive behavior that may accompany it, and look at our strengths that brought us together initially.

8. *Failure to repent and change.* Though it is wonderful and admirable to admit you are wrong, a healthy relationship needs more than that. We must seek forgiveness from the person we have wronged, be it spouse or child in the family. Repentance must come easily and naturally. After all, mortality is our first try at being a husband-father or wife-mother, so we are not experts. We are apprentices. Mistakes are going to be common and frequent. We are learning. Apologizing and moving past the problem are essential in righting relationships and carrying out elements of repentance. We ought to be sorry for our mistakes, but not martyrs. Sackcloth and ashes are out. We should simply make things right to the best of our ability. Once we feel genuine sorrow for any wrong we commit, have asked forgiveness, and made a sincere effort to correct our behavior, we both should be ready to move ahead (unless the mistake also requires Church action.)

9. *Failure to parent as partners.* JoAnn's children know that they have certain responsibilities in their home and that they cannot play with friends until their jobs are done. JoAnn sticks to this rule, and the children know it. Her husband, Ken, has a much more relaxed attitude, however. "Life is too hard to make them work so much when they are young. I had to work hard, and I hated it. Relax a little. Let them enjoy being young." When he is around, the children know they can either get out of doing their jobs or cause dissension between their parents. JoAnn feels angry at Ken for both undermining her authority with the children and not realizing the amount of help she needs to run the household.

Successful parenting requires a joint effort. It is critical that parents discuss their children as individuals and plan and be united in their child-rearing practices. If they don't, children learn to play one parent against the other. The

Lord has entrusted these spirits to our care because he has confidence that we can rear them—but we do it best when we work together as parents. Fathers often leave much of this work to the mother at home. He may help with the children grudgingly or even dutifully, perhaps with the feeling that he is graciously "helping out," and the wife knows that it will cost her something somewhere, sometime. He is mentally keeping track of his "goodness," and will remind her later of his "bank account balance." In actuality, his being intimately involved with the children and their activities is crucial to the healthy development of their children. And in a world where women are increasingly helping to support families, his responsibility may grow even larger in those homes. Regular talks and time with the children—lots of it—are essential to his developing his own parenting philosophy. (Some helps for dads are given in chapters nine and ten.)

10. *Poor money management practices.* Brent and Nichole, at the beginning of this chapter, are good examples of problems in this area. Nichole believed money was to be enjoyed and spent lavishly on whatever struck her fancy. Brent, on the other hand, worked hard to earn the money, and even though he was successful, he had very conservative feelings about how it should be used. Nichole's lack of control in money management and her indifference to Brent's feelings became, in his mind, justification for flirting elsewhere.

We often look around and naively suppose that those who have money are happy. Having all those wonderful possessions and trips must bring them happiness. And so we want all the wonderful things that are available to us— now. It's hard to be the only one who doesn't have a nice car or a computer or a new home. And so we often buy things without considering how to pay for them. The way we handle money is an extension of our personality, and often is a means of compensating for a lack of self-esteem. It could also be an indication of a power struggle in the marriage. Sometimes newly married couples get themselves into trouble trying to achieve the same standard of living as their parents have, not realizing it has taken their parents years to accumulate their assets. Some couples bury themselves in debt, and then turn on each other when they find the realities of repayment overwhelming. They blame each other for their financial predicament.

What we need to do is allocate our income carefully to our competing wants, after we take care of our needs. In today's economy, it is a challenge to make this match. We need some joint planning and the discipline of a workable budget. Making a spouse beg for money or spending so freely that we keep the family strapped are poor attitudes and likely trouble spots for any marriage.

11. *Different priorities.* This can occur in many different ways. How often do we see women bringing their children to church without their husbands? We can only guess at the pain and disappointment they feel. Spiritual matters are simply not top priority to some spouses, while their mates may feel an intense desire to participate in Church activities. I remember a woman who sneaked tithing to me as her bishop because her husband did not approve of such expenditures. I insisted she honor her husband's request; she insisted that she needed the blessings of the Lord. The division and disharmony that this type of situation fosters must be very difficult to deal with.

A friend felt extreme discouragement with her marriage, knowing that it had great potential but just was not living up to it. She began to concentrate her prayers towards finding help. Nothing developed for a long time, but she kept up her praying. Then she heard of a marriage seminar being held in her stake. She knew that her husband really disliked such activities and would likely refuse to attend. She felt desperately that this would offer them badly needed help. So she renewed her prayers, earnestly pleading for help to be able to approach her husband in a way that he could know of her sincerity and have a desire himself to improve their situation. After a week of prayer, she approached her husband. Nothing earthshaking happened, but he did agree to think about attending the classes I was teaching. She knew that it never could have happened if she had not prayed about it so intently. Because he related well with my presentation, we were able to follow up together in some further ideas and he has made some major modifications in his life—much to her delight. She also, though not aware of it at the time, was in need of some changes too. They began to communicate with each other and renew their relationship in ways that brought happiness to both of them.

Family unity and happiness must be top priorities. There are so many activities to pull a family apart today. Work, school, social activities, Church callings, sports—all can work wedges between us if we let them. Every spouse should ask, "How does my wife/husband really feel about me and our marriage? Am I meeting his/her needs and expectations of a marriage partner?" And every parent needs to ask himself, "What will my children, after they have left home, look back at with happy, warm feelings? Is our home a fun refuge from the storm, a haven to gather together in love to strengthen each other? If not, why don't I make it that way? What are the important things in our lives?"

Of course we all want to be happy. Sometimes we forget the simple things that contribute to marital happiness, or we complicate our family relations through selfishness and unhealthy interaction patterns. Humility, honesty, charity, and a willingness to teach and learn from each other are essential elements in marital happiness and stability.

Resolving Marital Problems 6

At the age of twenty-four, with a mission and much of my education behind me and with a wonderful wife by my side, I felt that I was in control of my life. I remember feeling confident in myself and my goals and the directions in which Geri and I were moving. We looked with anticipation toward the birth of our first child. I'll never forget the night that we drove to the hospital. I was anxious as my wife huddled in the front seat clutching a blanket and bravely trying to handle the pain. I felt, quite unexpectedly, rather helpless. Where was all my self-confidence? There were so many things that could go wrong—with her, with the baby. How often do you see your wife writhing in pain? What if she had the baby before I could get to the hospital? I thought to myself, *They used to die sometimes over this thing, didn't they?* My thoughts were racing. This emergency was very frightening, and yet thrilling at the same time, knowing that our family history was in the making. I suppose that nothing could have prepared me for the miracle and impact of the next few hours.

As I held our tiny baby boy in my arms, I was totally

unprepared for the feelings that flooded my soul. I thanked the Lord that I had made it to the Logan hospital in time, for my beautiful wife's safely passing through the "shadow of death," and for all the reality and wonder of conception, pregnancy, and birth. As I saw my little boy and the genetic stamp of my sweetheart and me, I was grateful for the principle of chastity—so appreciative that my wife and I had honored this sacred God-given trust. Now, David lay in my arms calmly looking back into my face, his eyes big, dark, and yet peaceful. I was amazed at the calm I saw there. What was going on in that little mind? How much could he understand, if anything? And suddenly, more than at any other time in my life, I wanted to be the best possible person, the best husband and father that I could be. I realized at that moment that I didn't have all the answers after all, that the cycle of life yet held many challenges. But, at that moment, I wanted to be a worthy son of God. Yes, I knew that I had a long way to go; but I also knew that for myself, for Geri, and for this little person, I wanted to go that long way. I wanted the Lord to be pleased with me as a husband and a father. That was my resolve.

Despite my personal commitment at that time, within six years of marriage my wife would tell me that she wasn't too thrilled with my performance as a father and that she was disappointed in our marriage. Somehow, though I had the desire to do right, and I loved my wife and children dearly, there were some gaps in my background that prevented me from fulfilling my dreams.

When we look forward to marriage and family relations with such great hope—as Geri and I did—what happens to two people to make them question their long-range commitment to each other? How could differences between two people become so insurmountable—sometimes rather suddenly—that they begin to wonder if their getting married was right? Does marriage differ that dramatically from dating and courtship that couples can go from the mountain peaks to the barren desert? Most couples, of course, make the transition to married life, but there are many who stagnate in emotional wastelands in which they reach only a fraction of their potential. The reasons have something to do with our background, our preparation for marriage, and our inability to translate gospel theory to practice within the context of family relations. I want to share some ideas with you about this.

My wife and I came from quite different backgrounds. I grew up in a family in which my parents were inactive and finally divorced. The reasons for the divorce were complex, but anger and impatience and strict discipline were common elements in my home. I was the youngest of two children and had no little brothers or sisters to play with and care for. Geri, on the other hand, came from a home where five children and two parents worked closely together in relative harmony. Her parents were of rather mild temperament. They did things together and there was a quiet closeness that has been their hallmark over the years.

After Geri and I married and we began our family, when our little children were noisy in church or defiant to my authority in any way, my orientation was to strongly discipline them, to spank them, to be harsh with them— just as I had been treated as a youngster. My wife's approach, on the other hand, was to talk quietly with them and teach them better ways to act. Obviously, the children preferred her way to mine and sought her out for help or counsel. I suppose, looking back on it, that I never did enjoy little children as a teenager. I thought they were noisy, messy, and unruly, and I just did not enjoy being around them. Yet I looked forward to being a father, and I assumed that my own children would be trained much differently than those I remembered. I had much to learn about building relationships with little ones. Even when you know the gospel is true and have served a mission, it takes a conscious, prolonged effort to translate gospel principles into calm, effective parenting practices—especially if that was not a part of your own growing-up years.

While Geri and I were dating, though, how could she possibly know what kind of a father I'd be for her children? And when it became obvious that I had trouble handling little children, how could she teach me and help me—unless I was humble enough to learn and really wanted to improve? At first I was defensive, thinking that she was too permissive, too lenient with them, and that they were manipulating and taking advantage of her. But over time, I learned that my children loved her, that she was patient with them, and that they responded to her methods better than mine. Most of their problems, as I think back on it, were a reflection of my negative reactions to them. In so many ways I was a poor teacher who had much to learn. Yet my wife had no evidence of my inadequacies as a father-to-be from simply dating me. When we are dating, there are many areas that are impossible to investigate. What can be done to deal with this problem? Here is a framework for understanding marital differences and ways to resolve them.

Role Theory

Role theory suggests that all of us play many different roles in our lives—student, teacher, athlete, employee, parent, customer, and so on. In fact, roles are the structure of the social fabric. Marital roles include those of spouse, sex partner, parent, therapist, housekeeper, provider, in-law, leisure-time manager, and religious practitioner.

Now, where do we learn to carry out behaviors that are considered "normal" or "typical" for these roles? As children we watch our parents perform these tasks, but we are rarely aware as to exactly *how* they perform most of them, or *how well* they carry them out. The parenting and housekeeping roles are probably the most obvious to us while the other roles are somewhat hidden. Gradually, however, we acquire role "norms"—ideas of what is right and wrong social behavior for these roles. We learn them at home, in school, through the media, and as we view the actions of other adults and parents of our friends. When we date, these roles become more prominent as we react to the "role performances" of our dating partners. We discuss and compare our experiences with friends who are also dating, and we generate expectations of how we and our dates should act. We formulate ideas about the type of physical and personality characteristics that we like in others.

As we move to the later teens and as the probability of marriage becomes a likelihood, family-life education takes an upward swing. We project ourselves carrying out dating, courting, and marital roles, and we imagine a partner in corresponding roles. A teenage boy, for example, thinks to himself: *It would be fun to be a husband, to be married, and come home every night to a cute wife; to have my own apartment, to have my back and neck rubbed; to read poetry to each other by the fireplace; and to be independent from the folks.* He thinks that being a husband won't be hard, after all. Girls, of course, fantasize themselves performing the female and wife roles very competently.

Other role expectations develop in a similar fashion. A boy attends fast meeting and watches a proud father bless his infant, who is then held up for the congregation's view, and decides that being a father will be fulfilling. He presumes that the provider role will take care of itself as he completes his education. He looks forward to the sexual and emotional dimensions of marriage. "After all," he figures, "it is fun to be affectionate now; imagine what sexual intimacy will be like!" He likewise concludes that his wife's parents will be supportive of him, she will keep the house spotless, leisure time will be available for his personal interests, and both will remain strong in their testimonies.

In effect, we anticipate the joys of marriage which we think have more appeal than simply dating—with its artificial and sometimes superficial overtones. Besides, by being married, we see ourselves as full-fledged adults. With the encouragement of friends traveling the same path, treating us as if we were already committed, we decide that we are ready for the leap. We convince ourselves that the Lord approves of this relationship or we would not have made it this far; and to clinch it all, we are going to marry in the temple!

Then, we ruin the dream by getting married! Soon we realize that we didn't go together long enough nor did we ask each other the right questions while dating. One of the problems in preparing for marriage is the fact that dating, especially short-term dating, does not allow much time for us to clarify our own role expectations, much less learn about those of a prospective mate, or even to know what they are. Dating is often a light-hearted experience where we try to impress each other with our "coolness." We are consciously displaying only our good traits, the positive personality dimensions that we want to show off. (I doubt if anyone has ever dated with the intention of displaying negative characteristics just so the other could see all facets of his personality.)

That is one reason why time is important in dating and courtship. Each person must have sufficient time to explore the personality and temperament of the other in a variety of realistic situations. How does this person react to stress? What kind of temper does he exhibit in times of crises? What about spiritual commitment to gospel principles? How does he treat his parents, brothers, and sisters? What demonstrations of affection and sensitivity are apparent in his family life compared with my own? What family or personal idiosyncrasies are revealed in his nature through a sampling of our interactions, and what is my response? What are his strengths and weaknesses? What are mine? Visiting each other's family to observe background traits that will surely play an important part in marriage should be mandatory! Some things should not be rushed but deserve adequate time, detailed observations, and lots of discussions.

The consequence of spending only limited time together before marriage can bring rather heavy penalties in the form of major adjustments after marriage. Judith Viorst has humorously portrayed this situation:

> Before my husband and I got married, we never had fights about anything. What was there, after all, to fight

about? On every fundamental issue—war, peace, race relations, religion, education, the meaning of the universe—we were in total, sweet accord. Surely we had no reason to think that this mellow state of affairs would not continue for the next 40 or 50 years.

From the moment we were married, we have managed to have fights about almost everything. What *isn't* there, after all, to fight about? We're still in total accord on those fundamental issues—but so what? That still leaves clothes, cooking, driving, sex, money, inlaws, children and who gets to read the newspaper first. And there isn't the slightest possibility that this embattled state of affairs will not continue.

I hadn't planned it this way. My marriage, as I all too frequently informed people in my premarital innocence, was going to be a mature, intelligent relationship. If, perchance, some small disagreement happened to trouble the serenity of our days, it would be resolved promptly by rational discourse. This was a swell plan.

Unfortunately, it had nothing much to do with reality. Reality, I found out in the course of our honeymoon, was my getting resentful about having to lend him my hairbrush and his getting huffy about the way I left the soap in the washbasin instead of in the soap dish. Honestly, I didn't know until then that we even *had* positions on hairbrushes and soap dishes—but we do indeed. Furthermore, we also have positions on tucking in the blanket at the bottom of the bed and serving meals on paper plates and putting records back in their jackets and turning off the lights. We have, it turns out, passionately held positions on hundreds of subjects too lowly ever to have been thought of until we started living, day in and day out, with someone who failed to share our cherished views.

He thinks a comfortable house temperature is 68 degrees. I think a comfortable temperature is 84.

He thinks a safe speed on the New Jersey Turnpike is 90 miles an hour. I think a safe speed is 45.

He thinks it's unnecessary to enter checks in the checkbook. I think that not entering each check should be punishable by death in the electric chair. . . .

Any couple is capable of escalating dumb disagreements to ferocious fighting. In our household, escalation often happens when it's too early in the morning or too late at night. Take 7:15 a.m., when, according to my youthful dreams, my husband and I were going to awake smiling warmly at each other, and then launch immediately into a vivacious discussion of [current events]. Instead, I grope my way out of bed feeling exceedingly crabby and put-upon, while he coldly informs me that there isn't a single pair of matching socks in his drawer.

Theoretically, it might be possible to respond with gracious good humor to this matutinal attack on my role as wife, mother and sex partner. Theoretically, it might even be possible to see his remark as something other than an attack. But 7:15 a.m. is not one of my finer moments—and it is definitely no time to talk to me about socks. So, I point out to him that just because his parents catered to all his infantile needs doesn't mean that I have to perpetuate this kind of crippling emotional dependency. The morning deteriorates from there. . . .

On countless occasions, in the afterfight afterglow, we both have made the most beautiful resolutions. I won't complain anymore when he's not on time. He won't complain anymore if I use his razor. I won't tell him he just went through a stop sign. He won't tell me I just destroyed the fried eggs.

For a full 24 hours we walk around the house suffused with the noblest feelings of tolerance and generosity, absolutely convinced that we will never fight again. We agree, do we not, on the fundamental issues? What is there, after all, to fight about. (Copyright © 1970 by Judith Viorst. Originally appeared in *Redbook*; condensed by *Reader's Digest*. Reprinted with permission from the November 1970 *Reader's Digest*.)

What married couple could not relate to this experience after a few months or years of marriage? There just isn't any way that a couple could possibly explore every role expectation prior to marriage.

This is not an uncommon experience for all of us. It occurs in practically every phase of our lives. Many young men and women, for example, project themselves into exotic careers—doctors, dentists, lawyers, and engineers. They see themselves beyond college, performing great feats of surgery, arguing legal principles before the bar, building giant engineering marvels, and, of course, being well-compensated for their expertise. However, as they begin their training in undergraduate work they learn that they must take Math 210 and Physics 205 as prerequisites. Suddenly the struggle, the reality of what is required in these basic courses on the way to fame and glory looms before them for the first time. Some of the luster is lost. They then must either dig in or change to some other major that doesn't require so much mental stress.

So, too, in marriage. Individuals come into marriage expecting to be competent marriage partners. They anticipate the satisfactions that marriage will bring. As they carry out their new roles, however, they soon discover that there are a number of areas that don't mesh. It is inevitable that such discrepancies arise. Just being male and female is sufficient difference to cause major shocks!

Even if an individual had the presence of mind during courtship to ask intelligent, practical questions, the answers would likely be rather idealistic. Think for a moment what kind of response would be given if one tried to gather more facts before marriage through a little snooping. Suppose, as a prospective wife, you were thoughtful enough to ask the following of your husband-to-be: "Dear, suppose we were married and I overdrew the checking account by twenty dollars. How would you react to that? What would you say to me?" Or, "Honey, suppose we were married and our little fifteen-month-old boy was fiddling around at breakfast and spilled the orange juice all over your new suit or on the carpet. How would you react to that? What would you say to our little Roger?"

The answers to such questions, if pursued, would, in all probability, be very objective and unemotional because they are not grounded in experience yet. We are all clear-thinking and objective when we are not emotionally involved. Any type of premarital quiz or test we could take at the time might be skewed in the direction of our being wonderful!

The more role discrepancies—differences between our expectations and actual performance—we encounter as marrieds, the more adjustments we face. The more important these discrepancies are, the more complicated the adjustments will be. Not replacing the toothpaste cap may not be a major problem compared with a husband not going to his Church meetings. Having a wife who is habitually late is not as critical as one who is unable to cope with motherhood (though "coping with motherhood" ought properly to include training children to be punctual). In general, the more important the role discrepancies are, and the greater their number, the more shocked we are at our own lack of preparation for marriage and wonder why we didn't anticipate those problems better before the ceremony.

As role discrepancies arise, however, it is time for charity and unselfishness to come into play; a time for understanding hearts and humility to draw two people together. It is a time to look at our personal and marital strengths. The temple commitment means that we accepted each other, knowing that we both had strong points and weaknesses that would be revealed in time. We committed ourselves to live the gospel and to work together to resolve any differences that surfaced. That, we reasoned then, was how we would grow and mature—by learning to communicate and help each other fill in any background gaps. Now the quality of our relationship is tested as we seek to work out satisfactory solutions.

President Spencer W. Kimball has written:

> Two people coming from different backgrounds soon learn after the ceremony is performed that stark reality must be faced. There is no longer a life of fantasy or of make-believe; we must come out of the clouds and put our feet firmly on the earth. Responsibility must be assumed and new duties must be accepted. Some personal freedoms must be relinquished and many adjustments, unselfish adjustments, must be made.

> One comes to realize very soon after the marriage that the spouse has weaknesses not previously revealed or discovered. The virtues that were constantly magnified during courtship now grow relatively smaller, and the weaknesses that seemed so small and insignificant during courtship now

grow to sizeable proportions. The hour has come for understanding hearts, for self-apprisal, and for good common
sense, reasoning, and planning. The habits of years now
show themselves; the spouse may be stingy or prodigal, lazy
or industrious, devout or irreligious, kind and cooperative or
petulant and cross, demanding or giving, egotistical or self-
effacing. (*Marriage,* pp. 35–36.)

Resolving Marital Role Discrepancies

Our marriage commitment presumes a willingness on
our part to learn how to be good companions, to enact
marital roles in ways that will benefit our family. And who
else is better qualified to help us understand the impact of
our actions than our mates and children. Since my wife,
for example, is directly affected by my role performances,
she is the one best able to help me learn how to improve,
to be a more effective husband, lover, therapist, and
father. And who knows most about the kind of homemaker, therapist, lover, and mother of my children that I
would like to have as my companion? I do, of course. Consequently, marriage is a profound commitment for us to
teach each other and provide some reactions and feedback
about how well we are doing.

Since we know little about each other when we marry
(because of the shallowness of dating), it is imperative that
we understand that marriage will test our ability to be
teachers and students in family processes. We will make
many mistakes and stumble as we try to become better
marriage partners. Many role discrepancies will not even
surface until we have been married for some time and we
are confronted by situations that we never anticipated
would develop. (Who could ever prepare ahead of time for
teenagers?) That is why Christlike traits—gentleness,
meekness, patience, kindness, forgiveness, tolerance,
cooperation—are so important for success in marriage.
When I share my views and feelings and needs with my
wife, she is more apt to understand and know how to help
me meet those needs as my therapist. The same is true
when I learn of her desires and want to strengthen her.

Problems arise in marriage because of our inability to be

students who are anxious to learn from the ones who can help us best, or because we are poor teachers. We teach through sarcasm, anger, punishment, or other negative ways. We fail to teach our family members in gentle, Christian ways. Many of us may be too stubborn, arrogant, or selfish to learn or to seek feedback on ways we can improve as marriage partners. We assume that our spouse should be able to read our mind, or should know what we need. But when we foster a spirit of learning and teaching, and we understand each other's needs, we can then use our agency to carry out our marital roles in ways that benefit the entire family.

We can all find gaps in the role performances of our spouse, but it is important that we do not become critical and intolerant. We all bring ingrained habits and tendencies with us into marriage that interfere with our effectiveness as a spouse or parent—if nothing more than sheer ignorance of the job. After all, these are new roles to us.

Changing Role Expectations and Role Performances

First, we can resolve role discrepancies by modifying or adjusting our role expectations. Soon after marriage we come to realize that the dating game has "faked us out" to some extent and that our preparation for some aspects of marriage were woefully lacking. We realize we were on our best behavior and so was our partner. We could see only the strengths then, but now we observe the appearance of some "freckles" that were heretofore unnoticed! We were somewhat naive in our perception and comprehension of the demands of marriage.

We may have even carried a "checklist" of the "perfect mate." If we were expecting to marry a "10," we soon learn that human beings do not come in that condition. (She turns out to be a 1.5 and we are but a .08!) We realize that some of our expectations were not only unfair, but were not really as important as we originally anticipated. Besides, there isn't much that can be done about physical traits—ankle size, hips, bust, hair loss, glasses, and such things. And as our love for each other matures, these features become less relevant—and hopefully more endearing. After thirty or forty years of marriage, we are all merely shadows of our former bodies anyway!

Second, and perhaps the most effective way to resolve role discrepancies, is to change the way we perform or carry out our roles. Marriage means we must be cooperative and helpful. A husband learns that his wife would like him to put his dirty clothes in the hamper rather than by the side of the bed, and that she would appreciate it if he would hang up his bathrobe, and leave the sink clean of shaven whiskers. She may even prefer that he carry his own plate from the table to the sink. Those acts are within his agency.

When a wife uses her fingernails on her husband's back, doesn't put her panty-hose in the sink where he shaves, and donates a few shoes to the Deseret Industries, that may please him. When neither one interrupts the other in conversation, when the husband initiates a consistent schedule of family home evenings and family prayer, when there are exchanges of love and affection, when each partner treats the other's feelings with sensitivity, when personal and family goals are monitored and carried out—when actions like these are the rule, they help create a healthy climate in which free agents can express their love for each other and do the little things that are so important to maintain marital well-being.

Couples who can't resolve differences by (1) changing role expectations or (2) changing role performances can "agree to disagree" or "avoid" certain areas of their marital interaction until such time that they can adjust, mellow, or pass on to the next life. Some couples never do resolve problem areas in their lives, but the differences are of such a nature that each understands that some divergence is okay, quite normal, perhaps healthy, and that such differences are easily tolerated. Some couples, for example, find that if the husband drives when they are together, they get along just fine. When the wife drives, however, friction develops because the wife seems insensitive to certain driving or mechanical norms, matters which are, for some reason, important to him. Couples may find that they are better off if they just avoid getting into situations that they do not handle well emotionally. Whether this is good or bad depends on the impact the avoidance has on the feelings of the individuals, whether there is a constant struggle over the matter that demands some resolution, or whether they can both be positive about it and even see some humor in their "solution."

Some of us are more prone to morning or night schedules, some need boards under the mattress to firm up the bed, or need Mentholatum in the nostrils at night to clear sinuses and breathing by morning, and we may have a number of unusual (to our partner at least) personal defenses and reactions in coping with mortality. One may have a certain phobia, or there are differences in taste and choice. There must be a mutual toleration of each other's idiosyncrasies. The "Dear Abby" column is full of such items. As we age, we see that our physical bodies don't perform as they once did. When we love each other, however, these frustrations are less of a problem and even provide us with some measure of comic relief.

To marry one who is not very humble or teachable, or one who thinks there is little contributed from you or your side of the family, will bring some challenging days to the marriage. In such cases, it builds resentment and then flexibility and adjustments are difficult. Such a marriage becomes a "one-up, one-down" relationship with one spouse insisting on the compliance of the other. If, on the other hand, humility prevails, and a sense of humor can lighten the journey, marriage adjustments become stepping-stones to greater love, trust, unity, and security.

Therefore, role discrepancies, though inevitable, need not constitute a threat to the progress of the marriage. In fact, they can be fun and humorous if we will see them as our unique personalities coming through. Surely the Lord doesn't expect us to have a perfect marriage at the commencement. However, we ought to be improving each year we are married, as we mature and increase in testimony of the plan of life, and as the importance of marriage and family grows in our hearts. After a few years we ought to be holding hands; after ten years we should even have our arms around each other; in fifteen we should be enjoying the kids the Lord sent us; at twenty years we should really be "falling in love"; after thirty our love is maturing and seasoning; after forty we start to look alike—have you noticed? And from there on in, we should be able to coast! Surely marriage is the great catalyst in helping each one of us develop Godlike attributes and traits. What a grand scheme God has instituted for our happiness and enjoyment. Unfortunately, marriage and family life, rather than making some individuals more Christlike, allows them to move in the direction of Satan. When abuse, anger, and infidelity destroy the sanctity of a home, hearts are broken and unhappiness results.

The following exercise provides an opportunity to seek feedback from each other as to how you are doing in marital role performance. Your spouse is your best source of feedback and help in improving. Be very charitable and gentle with each other as you review the roles given. Perhaps you two can see some ways to change and do things better. Do not go through them all at one sitting. Do only one or two at a time and be somewhat thorough. Remember you are helping each other to be more effective marriage partners. Learn from each other how to build your own exciting world.

Seeking Feedback in Marriage

Instructions: Pick out one role below and find out your spouse's reaction to the ways you carry it out in your marriage. Stay with it—don't escape until you have thoroughly investigated the topic together. The first sixteen deal with a husband's interest in how his wife feels about his roles; the next sixteen are for the wife to check out with her husband as to her role performance. The roles are labeled on the left. These are simply illustrations to help you get started. Do not go through them all at one time. Pick only one or two; try another at a later time.

Role		Husband Roles—Husband Asks Wife

Role   *Husband Roles—Husband Asks Wife*

Spouse 1. Honey, how do you feel about our marriage? Am I meeting your needs? Give me one suggestion that I can take to improve our marriage and make you happier.

Spouse 2. Do I have bad breath or dandruff, or other personal hygiene matters that concern you? Do you like my after-shave or cologne? whiskers?

Parent 3. Do you feel our children are growing up properly? Do you think I am doing my part to teach and work with them?

Parent 4. What is one way you see that I can improve as a daddy?

Parent 5. Do you feel that I spend enough time with the children?

Parent 6. Do you think I am too rough or too easy in disciplining the children?

Kinship 7. How do you feel about my family? Do you feel comfortable around all of them?

Housekeeping 8. Do you think that I'm helpful with the house jobs? What could I do to lighten your load in the home?

Recreation 9. Do you think we get out of the house often enough? How about as a family? Would you like us to do it more often?

Sexual 10. How do you feel about our intimate relations? What can I do to improve your satisfaction there? Am I careful? patient? Do you think there is enough foreplay and affection together?

Sexual 11. Do you feel that I am too demanding about sex in our marriage? Would you enjoy sex less often or more often?

Religious 12. Do you enjoy our ward? Relief Society? Who do you see as your closest friends in the ward?

Religious 13. Do you think that your faith has increased over the years? Do you think we could do more to study together or read some good Church books?

Therapeutic 14. When you really feel down, can you come to me with a problem? Do you feel that I am understanding and patient in listening and being helpful?

Therapeutic 15. Do you have thoughts or feelings that you find difficult to share with me?

Provider 16. How do you feel about our income level? Are you tired of our pinching all the time? Are there ways I can improve in my spending habits?

Role   *Wife Roles—Wife Asks Husband*

Spouse 1. Do I meet your needs as a wife? What is one thing that I could do to make your life more fun and enjoyable?

Spouse 2. What can I do to make myself a more interesting, fun companion? Do you feel comfortable with my weight? my clothes? Do you think that I wear too much makeup or not enough? Do you like my perfume?

Spouse	3.	Are there matters of personal hygiene that I should be more sensitive to? Does my breath smell bad on occasions?
Parent	4.	Do you see me as too permissive or too harsh with the children?
Parent	5.	How do you see me as a mother? Do you feel that the kids love me and that I am close to them?
Kinship	6.	Do you feel that your family likes me? What can I do to be more helpful or pleasing to them? Do you think I am too tied to my parents? Do you feel neglected because of them?
Homemaking	7.	Do you like the way our home is decorated? What can I do to make it more cozy and comfortable for you and the family?
Homemaking	8.	Do you like the food I prepare? Is there something you'd like me to have around the house more often to snack on, or a favorite food?
Homemaking	9.	Do you look forward to coming home from work? Am I keeping our home clean and tidy to your satisfaction? What should I do differently?
Sexual	10.	Am I meeting your needs in our intimate relations? Would you like me to initiate intimacy more often or less often?
Sexual	11.	If I didn't feel like being intimate on a particular occasion when you did, how could I let you know without your misunderstanding me that I am not rejecting you? I simply know that there are times when it is not comfortable for me. But I still love you.
Religious	12.	Am I supporting you in your priesthood assignments? home teaching? Do you like me to encourage you in carrying them out or does that bug you? Do you see it as nagging?
Therapeutic	13.	Do you feel comfortable in sharing your real thoughts and feelings with me? Can you risk easily with me? Do I ever interrupt you in an embarrassing way when you are talking?
Therapeutic	14.	Am I a good listener? Do you feel that I am good in helping you solve any problems or look for new ideas?
Provider	15.	Are you happy that I am home with the children, or do you feel that we have so much financial pressure that I ought to be out helping earn income?
Money Management	16.	Do you think I use money wisely in my share of our expenses? Do you think that I spend money on nonessentials?

Strengthening Emotional Bonds

The Lord intended marriage to be the most intimate of human relationships. "It is not good," the Lord declared, "that the man [or woman] should be alone; I will make him an help meet [companion]" (Genesis 2:18). As human beings, we naturally seek a companion, a confidante. We do not live our lives in a vacuum. Human beings were not meant to be hermits, detached and indifferent to others, but to be involved in relationships which will stir our divine potential. The quality of these relationships are developed and nurtured by our ability to communicate in ways that satisfy basic human yearnings for intimacy, expression, and acceptance.

We need an in-depth relationship with another, one who will be as a therapist through the trials and challenges of mortality. Marriage can bring the ultimate confirmation of each one's self-worth. An important cornerstone of personal mental health is the uniqueness and value we feel as individuals. In marriage we may come to know the very essence of another being—our spouse to whom we pledge our allegiance and a willingness to share practically everything—and to confirm our value as a son or daughter of God. This profound relationship gives significant meaning and purpose to our existence. Without it, we may shrivel and weaken.

Consider the marvel of marriage. Two people from possibly quite different backgrounds join together in a long-range commitment. They set up their housing and complement each other's needs for sexual and intimate contact. They secure the basic necessities for survival. They talk and listen; exchange ideas and values; share mutual hopes, dreams, and aspirations; and solve problems and challenges that arise as they meet life head-on. They risk their personal identities and forge a new oneness. They bear and rear children, who provide further experience for their mutual growth. The children then move out into the social matrix to find their own mates, and the cycle repeats. The basic unit of society, the family, becomes the means by which the social order is maintained and its values conveyed to the rising generation. In the process of family living, the opportunity to develop true intimacy exists. For those who do, it is the most thrilling of human experiences, the realization of true happiness. We thereby become complete, whole, and united in ways that are unattainable in any other relationship. For those who do not, it may become an overwhelming and crushing rejection of one's personality and meaning in life.

Communication is the vital process in human relations whereby marital bonds are forged and shaped and strengthened. It is the major tool that we may use to enhance and deepen our personal happiness and meet our quest for true intimacy.

Communication

The couple across from me shifted somewhat nervously. We visited for a while in an effort to relax, and eventually I asked the wife, "Sherrie, do you love Mark?" Her eyes dropped, she hesitated for a moment, and then she looked at me and said, "I don't know. I used to. My feelings for him have changed. In fact, I don't know whether I have any more feelings for him."

When Sherrie admits a loss of "feelings" for her husband, she is revealing a major breakdown of positive experiences and communication in the marriage. (Of course, all couples communicate, whether it is positive or negative. There is no such thing as couples not communicating.) But what she is saying is that positive exchanges, self-disclosure, and sharing personal ideas and opinions— so necessary for fostering and maintaining love emotions —has stopped or greatly dropped off. Personal needs are unmet. Communication, for them, has degenerated into negative, critical exchanges.

Communication carries a stimulus value that evokes feelings of varying intensity in us. We react to what others say in many ways—angrily, lovingly, or perhaps with some neutrality—depending on the context of the message. In marriage, we share our ideas and feelings with each other at several "levels of communication" which can promote (or hinder) emotional bonding. These "levels" refer to the quality and validating elements that occur in personal sharing, risking, and self-disclosure between marriage partners and between family members. The connection between these levels, our needs as human beings for attention and affection, and the development and strengthening of emotional bonds needs some discussion. Consider the following levels of communication:

1. *Superficial level.* This is a level of communication in which we spend much of our time in normal conversation. It is a relatively safe, nonargumentative, information-processing level. It is not a bad place to be, but not where you would like to spend your entire marriage. Topics tend to be light in nature, perhaps descriptive, and portray events or observations or narrations that require little investment of oneself. "It's a nice day, isn't it?" Unless we are meteorologists, we don't become emotionally involved in a reply. We simply respond to the common greeting and comments of others. "What did you think of the movie?" "Would you mind picking up some bread on the way

home?'' "Look at the hummingbirds feeding.'' Superficial comments represent statements with little risk on our part and the length of the conversation does not change the fact that the communication may be quite superficial. Superficial exchanges are important because they prepare the way, they lay a foundation, for greater self-disclosure if desired.

2. *Personal level.* At this level of communication we risk more of our personal ideas, opinions, and feelings—putting them on the line for inspection by others, willing to share with those whom we feel some measure of rapport and trust. We want and expect our personal views to be treated kindly and we guard ourselves against hurt or embarrassment. Our feelings on personal matters, private views on religion, politics, or philosophical positions may be topics that we hesitate to openly share with casual acquaintances, though the subject matter is less important than the depth of self-revelation. In marriage the personal level is a companionship level of exchange, and it is very important that both partners are able to risk personal thoughts and feelings with each other if emotional bonds are to develop.

3. *Validation level.* At this level, communication affirms the worth, value, and meaning of the other person. It is complimentary in nature. It is a way of expressing appreciation and love. It is always positive and may be either verbal or nonverbal. If I say to my wife, "I love being married to you; it's so fun to be your husband," I am expressing my regard for her. "I love you" messages are validating and are indispensable in marriage and family relations. A gentle touch, a squeeze of the hand, an embrace, a special look—all convey positive valuing of each other. Sexual intimacy, in marriage, is a very high form of validation, for it is a strong message of acceptance, love, and a combination of physical, emotional, and spiritual oneness.

Validation generally involves a greater level of risk than either the personal or superficial levels of communication because rejection is always possible when we risk our feelings. We are somewhat fragile and sensitive, and do not continue activities that are punishing. I asked Bill why he did not greet his wife Marilyn with a hug and kiss when he arrived home. He replied, "She would probably push me away, or think I was up to something." The fear of rejection was too painful for him to attempt an expression of love to her. Happy couples find it easy to validate each other, while couples struggling in marriage find it very difficult.

Human Needs

Abraham H. Maslow[1] theorized that human beings share common needs that he maintained were hierarchal in nature. He categorized them as follows:

1. *Physiological needs.* These include basic biological requirements for survival—food, air, water, clothing, and physical well-being. Each of us is motivated by self-preservation to meet fundamental biological needs.

2. *Safety or personal security needs.* We seek to be free from physical danger and to exercise some measure of control and predictability over our lives. We need a secure, steady environment to function near our potential.

3. *Social affiliation, love, and belongingness.* Human beings are social by nature, and we have a need to associate, to belong, to be a part of a common bond with others, be it in marriage, family, or a social group. We enjoy meaningful and fulfilling relationships with other human beings. When we feel shut out, ostracized, excluded, or unwelcome, we feel rejected and it is easy to become discouraged.

4. *Esteem needs.* Maslow suggested that though we have the need of affiliation, we also seek more than that. We want to be recognized and valued. We want to know that we are making a contribution to the lives of others, that our talents and personality are valued, that others

---

1. Maslow, *Motivation and Personality* (New York: Harper and Row, Publishers, 1954).

seek our ideas and association and help. We thereby develop feelings of self-confidence and personal worth.

5. *Self-actualization.* This means that we want to be ourselves, that we don't enjoy playing games or pretending to be something or someone we are not. We want to act in ways consistent with our core personality. We have faith that we can handle life's challenges. We desire to live life to the fullest extent we can.

Needs and Communication—The Integration

Now, let's integrate these last two concepts—basic human needs and levels of communication. Assuming that Maslow's formulation is fairly accurate, the question might be posed: "How do I as an individual satisfy my needs of belonging, esteem, and self-actualization on an ongoing basis in my life? The answer: *Through personal and validating levels of communication from those whose feedback I value*—my wife, children, friends, in-laws, employers, and similar persons. These two levels convey love, warmth, and value, and allow me to build a rapport with others in a way that generates feelings of acceptance, well-being, wholeness, and oneness.

What Sherrie was revealing about her marriage was the fact that there were few personal or validating exchanges going on with Mark. Their relationship had deteriorated to a superficial exchange of information, a much "safer" level for them to handle. However, with only superficial exchanges, few companionship and personal needs of love and belongingness are met. Of course, personal feelings and emotions die in such a sterile environment—much as a flower withers without water or sunlight.

How does my wife gain feelings that she is loved and appreciated for her role as a wife, mother, homemaker, confidante, sex partner? By my expressing, demonstrating, and communicating my love and appreciation for her. How does a husband receive esteem, love, and "positive strokes" for his efforts to support his family, to father effectively, and to be a loving husband? By his wife's and children's expressing their love to him for his influence in their lives. How do children, or any other human beings, have these basic needs fulfilled? Through the same process —receiving positive feedback from important others; then we feel valued as a person.

Now the mystery. When we understand this principle, why are we so stingy with love messages? Why don't we express appreciation and love for others more frequently? Why must we go to the funeral before we can say it? And then we speak only to the survivors. Why don't we express love directly, now, while those we love are still living and breathing. We could do much to lighten the load for many, not through insincere flattery but through simple gratitude and kindness. Marriage counselors see many people who are love-starved and crying out for some attention, some love, some positive message that says they are worthwhile.

Too often we use negative, critical communication to motivate the very ones we have invited to spend eternity with us. We all know that *we* function better when we receive praise and feedback for things we do well. Of course, situations arise in our families in which we must discipline and be firm, in which we must enforce the rules. But most of us are aware of our mistakes. Why must we embarrass others or make them pay the "uttermost farthing" when they make a miscalculation.

To review, meeting basic human needs occurs through our social interaction with others. When we receive positive feedback, feelings of love and worth are generated as social, esteem, and actualization needs are met by those in our "social network"—significant others—whose approval we value. When we exchange personal and positive messages, we contribute to each other's sense of worth and we function more effectively as human beings.

Recall David Mace's explanation of too little companionship in marriage:

> Some married couples live very superficially together. They communicate about routine matters, but do not share

their deepest thoughts. They live almost separate lives under one roof. They meet each other's elementary needs but never venture into what I call relationship-in-depth. Surprisingly enough, they may never even really get to know each other, because all they reveal is a limited area of their true selves. They simply live together on the basis of a mutual exchange of services. He "brings home the bacon," she takes care of the house; he takes care of the cars while she manages the children, etc. Based on a few such elementary exchanges, the marriage soon becomes dull and dreary.

Such mediocre marriages are very common in our culture. Yet often these very people are tormented by the longing for a relationship that is richer, deeper, and more meaningful. They are love-starved, and often they turn in other directions to seek what marriage has failed to give them. Sharing life in depth (with your spouse) is the solution to most of our human problems. (*Getting Ready for Marriage,* p. 68; emphasis added.)

This is not to say that healthy couples do not communicate at superficial levels. Of course they do. There is a great deal of information that needs processing in a family. In fact, the majority of our communication will probably be of this type. However, marriage partners who feel free to respond at any level consistent with their feelings are more happy, more at ease in marriage. Unhappy couples are unable to do that. They remain at superficial levels in order to avoid further antagonism or confrontation. When a married couple who are superficial with each other move to sexual intimacy (a high level of validation), generally strain is created in the relationship because the sexual union in this case is not a genuine reflection of mutual love, of true validation. It expresses hypocrisy, selfishness, and exploitation.

Superficial communication creates very little, if any, positive emotion or bonding between individuals, because so little of ourselves is offered in the way of interpersonal risk. First dates are a good example. Fred and Gina have a tough time making conversation, exhausting myriad topics looking for common ground and common values that can help put them at ease and on more intimate terms.

(Next time Fred vows he will go to a movie—it's much safer than facing her over dinner. But there is little likelihood of an emotional attachment forming if Fred and Gina struggle with a superficial level.)

Let's test this principle right now in your marriage. Go to your companion, touch or embrace him, look him in the eyes, and say gently, "Honey, I just felt like telling you how much I love you. Thanks for being my sweetheart. I love you and I love being married to you." Now kiss him. (If you were unable to do this, analyze why you couldn't. What stopped you? Now you know what this chapter is all about. If he is absolutely shocked, that says something too, doesn't it?)

The following table summarizes the relationship between different levels of communication and the development of feelings and emotions.

Positive Communication Levels	*Emotional Bonding— Satisfaction of Personal Needs*
Superficial	Low
Personal, companionship topics	Moderate to high
Validation: Verbal	High
Nonverbal (touch, voice, eyes)	High
Sexual intimacy in marriage	High

Let's go back to Sherrie and Mark at the beginning of the chapter. Sherrie commented on the loss of feelings for Mark. Obviously, little or no personal validation was being exchanged. They were unhappy. Positive feelings and emotions for each other had evaporated, and their relationship was in jeopardy. It would be impossible for Sherrie to say, "I know we are having some problems, dear, but I love you with all my heart." When validation ceases, love feelings are soon snuffed out. To safeguard their own mental health, Mark and Sherrie resorted to shutting down any positive signals and withdrew from each other in fear of further rejection.

They became hostile, distant, and defensive with each

other. They blamed each other for their difficulties; their sexual relations became less rewarding or nonexistent. Their relationship was frustrating both of them. Here's a typical attempt to communicate, which they shared with me.

Mark was lying on the couch watching a baseball game. Sherrie approached, wanting to talk over a few things. Mark didn't even look at her as she entered the room. She said, "Mark, we've got to talk."

"Do I have any choice in the matter?" he responded.

"If you had your way we'd never speak to each other at all. What kind of a marriage is that?"

"Well, if you had your way we'd be confronting each other every minute. That's not my idea of having fun."

"Well, confronting is better than ignoring each other."

"You make it so hard."

"Do we have to go through this again?"

"If you don't talk to me, we might just as well kiss this marriage good-by."

"Maybe that's just what we should do."

This conversation might be repeated in many homes when feelings are stirred in a marriage. But what poor responses! It is a reaction based on pride and arrogance, not humility. This is not the type of behavior that covenant people seeking the celestial kingdom exhibit. Can you imagine heavenly parents reacting to each other that way? In reality Mark and Sherrie are violating major commandments as well as their marriage covenants. Not much personal or validating communication going on here, is there!

Now is the time for Mark and Sherrie to repent, to stop hurting each other with negative, uncharitable comments. They need to get their heads and hearts right. It must be obvious to any outsider, and hopefully to them, that they are living without the Spirit of the Lord in their lives. Mark and Sherrie must repent by taking responsibility for their own remarks, apologizing, freely asking and extending forgiveness and recommitting themselves to each other. They must try again, exercise better self-control, change their negative behaviors and reactions, please each other, and make an effort to rekindle their companionship and mutual feelings. In offending each other they have also offended their Heavenly Father.

"But," one might ask, "how can you make changes when someone else is hurting you?" That, of course, is what the gospel is all about. This question is one the world asks in its competitive, self-justifying way. But it is not what Latter-day Saints are about. It might help to remember the Savior's great example. On the cross, while experiencing unbelievable pain and suffering, he pleaded for forgiveness in behalf of his enemies. Manifesting charity to the end, Jesus was in complete control of his head and heart because of his perspective of his earthly and heavenly mission. He understood his role and his mission, while those putting him to death had no such perspective. He could even be compassionate at a time like that. He knew that he was born into the world for that very purpose.

Though it is difficult for us as fallen beings to maintain this perspective and always act with charity toward others, we must learn to do so if we expect to be his disciples. We must not allow our relationships to slip and sink to such a state that we are abusive to each other; after all, we understand the gospel, and we hold the priesthood and represent the very God of heaven. President Ezra Taft Benson outlined the correct perspective:

> As I have listened to these reports [of wife and child abuse], I have asked myself, "How can any member of the Church—any man who holds the priesthood of God—be guilty of cruelty to his own wife and children."
>
> Such actions, if practiced by a priesthood holder, are almost inconceivable. They are totally out of character with the teachings of the Church and the gospel of Jesus Christ.
>
> As priesthood holders, we are to emulate the character of the Savior. . . .
>
> Whenever a priesthood holder departs from the path of virtue in any form or expression, he loses the Spirit and comes under Satan's power. . . .

A priesthood holder who would curse his wife, abuse her with words or actions, or do the same to one of his own children is guilty of a grievous sin. . . .

If a man does not control his temper, it is a sad admission that he is not in control of his thoughts. He then becomes a victim to his own passions and emotions, which lead him to actions that are totally unfit for civilized behavior, let alone behavior for a priesthood holder. . . .

As I've thought about the serious sins that some of our brethren have committed, I've wondered, "Did they seek the Lord to help them overcome their emotional outbursts? Did they rely on fasting and prayer? Did they seek a priesthood blessing? Did they ask our Heavenly Father to temper their emotions by the influence of the Holy Ghost? . . ."

Your wife is your most precious and eternal helpmate—your eternal companion. She is to be cherished and loved.

There are only two commandments where the Lord tells us to love someone with all our hearts. The first you are familiar with as the Great Commandment: "Thou shalt love the Lord thy God with all thy heart, and with all thy soul, and with all thy mind." (Matthew 22:37.)

The second commandment to love another with all our hearts is this: "Thou shalt love thy wife with all thy heart, and shalt *cleave unto her* and none else" (D&C 42:22). . . .

You should always remember the statement of the Savior that "the spirit of contention is not of me, but is of the devil." (3 Ne. 11:29.) Never allow the adversary to be an influence in your home. . . .

. . . We should be as charitable and considerate with our loved ones as Christ is with us. He is kind, loving, and patient with each of us. Should we not reciprocate the same love to our wives and children? (*Ensign*, Nov. 1983, pp. 42–44.)

I wonder how different Mark and Sherrie's conversation might have been if each was pleading in personal prayer for patience, for greater self-control, for the ability to change actions; if each was humble and grateful for the privilege of marriage and could see that both had strengths as a couple. Suppose Mark had responded to Sherrie's initial approach with "Your voice sounds like you're upset with me; have I done something dumb?" Instead of protecting himself or avoiding a discussion with her, he could show a willingness to try, to be interested in her concerns. The quality of the relationship is a top priority—now, always. And if Sherrie tempered her heart, her approach would not be so combative, and she would approach her husband in a way that would convey love—even when she felt the need to tackle a serious problem.

We are free agents. Though it may take every bit of spiritual strength we have, we *can* be pleasant and non-defensive in our communication. We *can* keep our mouths closed when we need to listen. I will not say that it is easy, but I can vouch for a better result in the long run when we try. If we are to be the Savior's disciples, we must keep our hearts gentle and in tune with the Spirit of the Lord, and not resort to tactics clearly modeled in the world—anger, rationalization, self-betrayal, excusing oneself, and blaming others.

President Spencer W. Kimball explained how some problems develop in families and gave a way to make needed corrections:

> Sometimes the husband or the wife feels neglected, mistreated, and ignored until he or she wrongly feels justified in adding to errors. If each spouse submits to frequent self-analysis and measures his own imperfections by the yardstick of perfection and the Golden Rule, and if each spouse sets about to correct self in every deviation found by such analysis rather than to set about to correct the deviations in the other party, then transformation comes and happiness is the result. There are many pharisaic people . . . who prate their own virtues and pile up their own qualities of goodness and put them on the scales against the weaknesses of the spouse. . . .
>
> For every friction, there is a cause; and whenever there is unhappiness, each should search self to find the cause or at least that portion of the cause which originated in that self. (*Marriage*, pp. 42–43.)

We all need frequent large doses of validation in our lives. When an individual learns that he can risk his own feelings with a spouse or children, a therapeutic environment is established in the home. Healthy married couples risk openly and respond to each other positively. Consequently, trust, charity, and love flow between the members of such a marriage.

Companionship, expressing love, trying to please, the development of self-esteem as God's children, repenting, and using our agency with self-discipline—these are fundamental elements of happiness. The plan of salvation is grounded in these principles. The Savior taught us to love one another. He loves us in spite of our weaknesses. The very core of our self-worth is the profound truth that as God's offspring, we have unlimited potential. When we see that relationship to him, we can self-actualize to the highest extent!

People marry with the expectation that they will experience a deep level of fulfillment of their personal needs through marital companionship and intimacy. How thrilling family life can be when people frequently risk positive validation with each other through expressions of love. Many problems in family relations could be resolved if we were more positive and supportive of those with whom we live.

In the following lists—"Improving Our Personal Level of Communication," "Learning Validation Processes," and "Deepening Our Love Commitment"—are some aids to developing a greater ability to communicate at personal and validating levels. They contain some suggestions on ways to improve marriage—little things we can do to make life more fun. Look at them carefully and make of them whatever application you can in your own marriage.

Improving Our Personal
Level of Communication

Every evening prior to bedtime, please take one of the topics below and spend at least fifteen minutes discussing it together. Try to relax with each other and be genuine in your feelings and sharing.

1. When I first knew that I loved you and wanted to marry you.
2. How I feel about myself—my own strengths and weaknesses.
3. Things that make me feel happy—activities that I really enjoy doing with you.
4. How marriage has been different from what I anticipated in the beginning.
5. An outstanding trait that I think you have developed in our marriage.
6. My favorite scripture, poem, or anecdote.
7. The most spiritual experience that I have had in my life.
8. How I feel about being a mom or dad.
9. The meaning of sexual intimacy to me and the part I thought it would play in my marriage.
10. How I feel about my career or homemaker role.
11. The best part of being married to you from my point of view.
12. Where I got my attitudes about money/debt/spending.
13. What depresses or frustrates me most in life.
14. What trait I like in other people that I would most like to have.
15. One area that I need some help in improving in my own roles.
16. How I feel our children are doing in various areas of their lives.
17. The most important need I have in our marriage.
18. How I feel about the gospel—the strength of my own testimony now compared with my early years.
19. One time I really got angry with you (and how that got resolved).
20. How I feel about my own family—parents, brothers and sisters, etc.
21. What I like and dislike about my own appearance.
22. What personality characteristic I would really like to have.

23. If we got a windfall of $1,000, what would you like us to do with it?
24. What I would really like us to do more than anything else in the world.
25. What I have learned by being married to you.
26. What time in my life was the most growth-producing.
27. If we could go on a vacation, I would like to take the family, or you and me . . .
28. One thing my parents did as I was growing up that I always wanted to do with our family is . . .
29. If I could be twenty, thirty, forty, or fifty again, knowing what I know, I would . . .
30. One area that I have tried to overcome all my life is . . .
31. Over the years I think that my temper has . . .
32. It has been so much fun to have children. I didn't know that over the years I would feel toward them so . . .
33. If I were to go to college again, I would study . . .
34. If we were to start our marriage over again, this time I would be sure to . . .
35. If you were ever called to be bishop (Relief Society president), I would feel . . .
36. I think that the best place we could live on the whole earth is . . .
37. List other topics important to you and discuss them together.

Learning Validation Processes

What do the following actions or phrases really say in a positive, validating way?

1. A husband picks up his clothes regularly, makes the bed, and does some dishes.
2. A husband reads the little ones a story and puts them to bed.

3. A husband changes the baby's diaper and even gets up at night to feed a non-nursing baby. If his wife is nursing the baby he often visits or reads to her.

4. A wife asks her husband's help on preparing a Relief Society or Primary lesson.

5. A husband gathers up the children to take them on an errand to allow his wife some time to herself.

6. A husband says, "Now, don't worry—I'll take care of the house and the children while you are out."

7. A wife greets her husband at the door with a hug and kiss and says, "I just love it when you come home. I've missed you all day and can't wait to see you."

8. A wife says: "Oh, I don't want to go if you don't want to. It's no fun without you."

9. A wife showers, puts on her negligee and his favorite perfume.

10. A husband showers, shaves, and puts on her favorite cologne.

11. A husband says, "Honey, let me explain what is happening. The quarterback gets the ball from the center, and . . ."

12. A husband asks: "Is there anything I can do to help you with supper?" or "help you with the kids?"

13. A husband volunteers: "It's my turn to do the dishes—you go and relax."

14. "You are so patient in helping the children. They love you so much—I can see it in their eyes. That makes me love you all the more."

15. "I didn't know when I married you that you were going to be such a great companion. I just love being married to you."

16. "I love going to the temple with you—it reminds me of when we were married."

17. "I remember before we got married wondering to myself, 'Will I love her/him in five years as I do now?' Now I know I didn't even know what real love was then."

18. "When you call our family together for family home evening or family prayer, it really makes me happy."
19. A wife tells the children: "Let's go see what Daddy thinks we ought to do about that."
20. A husband reports: "I made reservations for dinner, and Jane is coming over to babysit for us."
21. The husband washes and cleans his wife's car.
22. "It was so much fun to be alone with you tonight for dinner and the play."
23. "It is so much fun being married to you. I think this is the happiest time of my life."
24. A husband rubs his wife's feet and back at the end of the day.
25. "I really appreciate your sharing your thoughts and ideas with me. Sometimes I feel that we don't talk enough together, but I really love to hear you express your feelings to me."
26. The husband takes the vacuum cleaner out and cleans up his cheese and cracker crumbs or wipes the tablecloth off after spilling the milk.
27. The husband gets up and gets his own drink of water or ketchup from the refrigerator.
28. A husband says: "Honey, I have some time today—what would you like me to help you with?"
29. "I didn't realize I was so dependent on you until you were gone for a week on that business trip."
30. "What I really like is to have you come home from work and take some time to play with the kids before supper. That is my best time of the day."

Any action or statement that conveys: "You are important to my happiness and make me feel loved and appreciated—that is how happy marriages are sustained."

Deepening Our Love Commitment

Things a husband can do:

1. Embrace your wife with a kiss when you arrive home. Plant a good one on her.

2. Counsel with her on business as well as personal matters. You'll find her wise in many ways.
3. Bring her flowers while she can still smell them.
4. Use the same good manners with your spouse that you would with a client out on the golf course.
5. Even if you've been married a long time, compliment her on her cooking and homemaking skills.
6. Remember that tenderness is important to women. Be sensitive to her feelings and be romantic rather than macho.
7. Bring her nice things home for no reason other than that you love her.
8. Compliment her on her mothering skills, and be specific.
9. When she is telling a story, don't give away the punch line or take it over.
10. Provide her with some funds for which she does not have to account or explain.
11. Never, never ask: "What have you done all day, dear?"
12. Share with her things that you love most about her, frequently.
13. Surprise her with a night off from the kitchen—you do the cooking or take the family out for dinner. Use coupons and two-for-ones—and spend time as a family.
14. When dinner is over, help her clean up the dishes and share the good things that happened during the day, or ask her help on a matter.
15. Take the kids on an errand or out in the yard to play —give her a chance to relax.
16. Make a date and you arrange for the babysitter and the tickets.
17. Take the baby or little one out when he/she cries in a church or other meeting.
18. Ask your wife for one suggestion as to how you ought to improve as a husband/father—and do it.
19. Bathe the kids and put them to bed while your wife relaxes.

20. Remember that your wife has never been a wife before. Express to her those things she does well—she will then learn how to satisfy and please you and enjoy her job.

21. Be sensitive to your wife's sexual needs. She has the right to have her own needs met. There will be times you will need to exercise self-control in her behalf.

Things a wife can do:

1. Your spouse has never been one before—so help him to understand what you like him to do by shaping his behavior to bless you and your family.

2. Don't tell him the day's problems until you've fed him. If it's a real disaster, like taking off the fender of the car, make the dinner an especially favorite one.

3. Buy a new nightgown, don't charge it to him, and wear it often.

4. Write him love notes once in a while for his lunch box, pocket, or scriptures.

5. Provide a comfortable home where he can relax and spend some private time.

6. Don't make him the family "meany." Don't say to the children, "Just wait until your father gets home," or "I want to let you, but Daddy says no."

7. Remember the things you said and did to land him in the first place—do them again.

8. Don't shush your husband if he sings at ward parties or acts like a clown at times.

9. Don't be on the telephone when he comes home, and don't start talking on the phone until he leaves for work. Be home when he comes home.

10. Share with him that which you love most about him.

11. If he usually initiates love and affection, turn the tables frequently. Initiate hugs and kisses with him.

12. Pay cash for his presents—don't buy him a gift and then charge it to him.

13. When he brings home a mess of fish or wild game—

no matter how unappetizing—cook them to the best of your ability and eat them.

14. Don't keep asking him, "Do you love me?"
15. Remember to record the checks you wrote today. Keep your check register up to date.
16. You take the baby-sitter home occasionally.
17. Don't borrow his razor.
18. Ask your husband for one suggestion, something he would like to have you do differently to improve as a wife and mother—and do it.
19. Remember that happily married people enjoy frequent sexual relations. There will be times when your husband is discouraged or frustrated and he will need your love.
20. Be a good co-leader in your home. Ask your husband's suggestions on items and keep a good calendar of family activities and events. Review them regularly.

What you both can do together:

1. Don't call each other Mother and Father, and stay away from couples who do—unless you are in your eighties!
2. If you say your prayers together before you go to bed, you'll have your thoughts on something higher than yourselves and your problems. Pray for each other.
3. Read some scripture together and have a good gospel discussion.
4. Share your spiritual experiences (Relief Society, priesthood meeting, home teaching, temple, scripture study, etc.).
5. Take up a challenging sport or hobby that you can do together—skin diving, tennis, water or snow skiing, mountain climbing or hiking, jogging (with physician's consent).
6. Stop trying to keep up with the Joneses—about the time you make it they'll refinance.

7. Be positive with each other and the children. Compliment each other on body and looks.

8. Avoid getting mad at the same time. Avoid getting mad at all—the only time you should raise your voice is when the house is on fire!

9. Meta-communicate—that is, talk together about how you "talk together."

10. Respect each other's privacy and modesty.

11. Take the family on a one-day excursion in the area. Pack a picnic and enjoy the day.

12. Work together on a civic or community project.

13. Don't sacrifice all your fun today for what you think is security tomorrow.

14. Spend the night at a motel or hotel—at least once a year on your anniversary.

15. Make a family picture album together.

16. Spend one night out each week as dating partners. Remember that a babysitter is cheaper than a divorce.

17. Switch off the TV and have a good discussion about each child in your family.

18. Always have some project going for you—something to do, build, buy, or a place to travel. Save some money out of each paycheck for a trip together.

19. Drop the words I, me, and mine from your vocabulary and use we, us, and ours.

20. Build each other up in public. Don't compete with each other. You are one now.

21. Never, never criticize each other—not in public or private. You are not married to a parent, but to your spouse.

22. Never begin a sentence with "It seems to me a good husband would...," or "A good wife would...," or "After all I've done for you . . ."

23. Jointly work on your genealogy.

24. Read each other's patriarchal blessing occasionally to appreciate the potential in each other. (Your task is to make sure your spouse gains exaltation.)

25. Put a lock on your bedroom door.
26. Have dinner at home alone together after the children are in bed; or go for a treat together, or fix one at home.
27. Watch a late movie together—and stay awake in each other's arms.
28. Get a remote controlled TV and mount it on the wall in your bedroom and watch some news and movies together in each other's arms.
29. Don't neglect each other for the children's sake.
30. Write to the temple president (or the one who married you) and thank him for getting you off to a good start.
31. Bring your family journal up-to-date by recalling events together since marriage.
32. Check with each other as to your marital satisfaction —things you can do to improve your family relations.
33. Begin putting money away now for a mission together later.
34. Keep romance in your marriage by doing little things that convey love and appreciation.
35. When you finish reading all of these items, give your spouse a big hug and kiss.

Intimacy in Marriage

8

Validation, as I presented it in the preceding chapter, is an emotion-building communication level, and in marriage it is an important expression of love and commitment. Sexual intimacy is a particularly powerful means of validation designed to let us share our love with each other as marrieds in a way that we share it with no one else.

Historically, social attitudes about sexual behavior have been out of harmony with the gospel. One of the oldest, Satan-inspired perspectives has been the notion that sex is unholy and ungodly but necessary to propagate the species, that sexual passion is the basic source of our alienation from God and the primary obstacle to the development of spirituality. If not outright sinful, sex was considered detrimental to man's spiritual progress.

This negative philosophy probably dates back to Plato and St. Augustine. It viewed the body as the principal barrier in man's struggle to "overcome the flesh." Philosophies that honored the mind but debased the body saw fallen man as inherently anti-spiritual. "Passions of the flesh" prevented man from rising to his full stature before

God. This perspective has never quite disappeared from men's thinking.

A bold and current perspective known as "situational ethics" or "permissiveness with affection" views premarital intimacy as acceptable as long as "no one gets hurt" or as long as some "love" exists between two consenting adults. Sexual intimacy is neither right nor wrong for unmarrieds, this reasoning goes, unless the outcome is negative—unwanted pregnancy, disease, exploitation, or selfishness. Television and movies frequently portray this image.

For Latter-day Saints the commandment governing sexual powers is simple: sexual intimacy is reserved for marriage. The Lord authorizes the use of procreative powers only in marriage—for a man and wife to bring children to the earth, for mutual comfort and therapy between the two, and as a profound expression of their spiritual, emotional, and physical love and commitment. President Spencer W. Kimball has expressed his dismay at the sexual permissiveness of the day:

> Libraries are loaded with books with shocking pictures, showing people how to totally satisfy their animal natures. . . . With a theory that "life is for sex," every imagination of the minds of men devises ways to more completely get what they call "sexual fulfillment," which they demand at the expense of all else—family, home, eternal life. (*Ensign*, June 1971, p. 17.)

Mormon doctrine contributes a broad base for understanding the basic nature, purpose, and sanctity of this great human endowment. Our belief is that procreation, the power to create life, is an earthly stewardship that may extend beyond this life if we are faithful. In fact, our theology is clear that we, ourselves, are the literal offspring of parents who have this very power. Brigham Young observed: "Man is the offspring of God. . . . We are as much the children of this great Being as we are the children of our mortal progenitors. We are flesh of his flesh, bone of his bone." (*Journal of Discourses*, 9:283.)

In our premortal life, we each had an individual identity as a male or female spirit. Since our parents there were not subject to death, our spirit bodies are inherently immortal. Coming to earth, however, we gain another body, a mortal one, as a counterpart to the spirit body. This body is composed of the elements of this fallen earth and is organized by the process of procreation. Since our earthly parents, Adam and Eve, fell, our bodies are subject to dissolution and death.

In the post-resurrection life, however, if we achieve exaltation, we may regain the ability to propagate children —spirit children, in this case. Those in the lower kingdoms of glory will lose that power and nature. President Joseph Fielding Smith explained:

> Some will gain celestial bodies with all the powers of exaltation and eternal increase. . . . In both of [the lower] kingdoms there will be changes in the bodies and limitations. They will not have the power of increase, neither the power or nature to live as husbands and wives, for this will be denied them and they cannot increase. . . . Some of the functions in the celestial body will not appear in the terrestrial body, neither in the telestial body, and the power of procreation will be removed. (*Doctrines of Salvation*, Bruce R. McConkie, comp. [Salt Lake City: Bookcraft, 1955], 2:287–88.)

Even in the celestial kingdom there will be some restrictions:

> Restrictions will be placed upon those who enter the terrestrial and telestial kingdoms, and *even those in the celestial kingdom who do not get the exaltation;* changes will be made in their bodies to suit their condition: and there will be no marrying or giving in marriage nor living together of men and women, because of these restrictions. (*Ibid.*, p. 73; emphasis added.)

As already quoted, the Doctrine and Covenants (131:1–4) confirms that in the resurrection those who do not gain exaltation will not be married nor will they continue parenthood.

It is apparent from these statements that sexual powers, though they are lost in death, may again be restored to mankind in the resurrection. The celestial body will have the functional endowment of procreation similar to our experience here on earth, except that there we organize eternal spirit beings:

> What do we mean by endless or eternal increase? We mean that through the righteousness and faithfulness of men and women who keep the commandments of God they will come forth with celestial bodies; . . . and unto them, through their preparation, there will come spirit children. I don't think that is very difficult to comprehend. The nature of the offspring is determined by the nature of the substance that flows in the veins of the being. When blood flows in the veins of the being the offspring will be what blood produces, which is tangible flesh and bone; but when that which flows in the veins is spirit matter [as is true with resurrected beings], a substance which is more refined and pure and glorious than blood, the offspring of such beings will be spirit children. (*Melvin J. Ballard—Crusader for Righteousness* [Salt Lake City: Bookcraft, 1966], p. 211.)

In short, parenthood is the greatest gift God can bestow on his glorified children, a privilege which is possible through faithful observance of the laws of marriage. Perhaps in marriage and family relations we most closely approximate and imitate the heavenly pattern.

Chastity, meaning abstinence from sexual activity prior to marriage and fidelity after marriage, is an integral part of God's plan for focusing the great powers of sexuality into the Godlike callings of partnering and parenting. Chastity is a commandment that God requires his children to obey, and he has made it clear that unauthorized cohabitation and sexual intimacy between unmarrieds is absolutely forbidden. President Spencer W. Kimball voiced the rule that "there should be total chastity of men and women before marriage and total fidelity in marriage" (*The Teachings of Spencer W. Kimball*, p. 264).

One of the great tragedies Church leaders and counselors face is the misuse of these sacred powers in and out of marriage. Adultery is devastating to the kind of marriage the gospel teaches. Not only is repentance long and difficult, but the fragile thread of trust between companions, once broken, is often difficult if not impossible to restore. Little wonder that the prophets have taught that a man or woman who cannot be true to sacred moral covenants is endangering his or her eternal life. Breaking the heart of one's spouse or stopping one's own progress through infidelity is a sin of major consequence.

On the other hand, a husband and wife, in pledging total fidelity to one another, develop a profound trust that neither will offend God nor break personal covenants through immoral actions. Such covenant persons will find, as they move about in their environment, that temptations have little or no lasting effect on them, because their covenants with God and their companion provide them with the power to resist any diversion from their eternal goals.

Alma indicated that there are only two crimes more serious than that of sexual sins. They are (1) the sin against the Holy Ghost, which makes one a son of perdition, and (2) murder, the intentional taking of another's life. (See Alma 39:5.)

The First Presidency taught:

Sexual sin—the illicit sexual relations of men and women—stands, in its enormity, next to murder. . . . The Lord has drawn no essential distinctions between fornication and adultery and harlotry or prostitution. (Quoted in Roy W. Doxey, *Latter-day Prophets and the Doctrine and Covenants*, 4 vols. [Salt Lake City: Deseret Book Company, 1978], 2:16–17.)

All sexual sins are serious because they represent a desecration and mockery of the very powers of Deity.

Few individuals will become sons of perdition, and few Latter-day Saints will ever be tempted to the point of taking another's life. Perhaps the greatest danger that a Latter-day Saint faces as regards the possible loss of salvation is in this area of moral transgressions. Perhaps that is why Satan is putting so much emphasis on destroying, if possible, those who have the very powers which he is eternally denied. It is true that, given repentance, the Atonement may expiate such moral sins, but forgiveness is not easy to obtain. Little wonder that prophets have continually warned the Saints about carelessness in this area wherein our eternal life is at stake!

Joseph Smith once observed: "If a man commit adultery, he cannot receive the celestial kingdom of God. Even if he is saved in any kingdom, it cannot be the celestial kingdom." (*History of the Church*, 6:81.)

That is a stunning statement which deserves some explanation. In context, the Prophet made the statement in the presence of several Apostles in his home in Nauvoo. Apparently it does not apply to an individual member of the Church who does not have his calling and election made sure. (See McConkie, *Mormon Doctrine*, pp. 24–25.) However, this statement does impress us with the impact of the seriousness of this sin. (See President Spencer W. Kimball's discussion of the Prophet's statement in *The Miracle of Forgiveness*, [Salt Lake City: Bookcraft, 1969], pp. 346–50.)

The scriptural blessing or cursing given by the Lord is impressive: "This is eternal lives—to know the only wise and true God, and Jesus Christ, whom he hath sent. . . . Broad is the gate, and wide the way that leadeth to the deaths; and many there are that go in thereat, because they receive me not, neither do they abide in my law." (D&C 132:24–25.)

Eternal deaths, in contrast to eternal lives, refers to the loss of "lives" suffered by those who might have been eligible for eternal increase but who did not live worthy of such privileges.

Sometimes the ban against sexual relations outside of marriage is stressed so strongly in Church meetings—and rightly so—that the impression may be left that anything less than sexual intercourse may not constitute sinful behavior. Again, President Kimball soberly declared:

> Among the most common sexual sins our young people commit are necking and petting. Not only do these improper relations often lead to fornication, pregnancy and abortions

—all ugly sins—but *in and of themselves they are pernicious evils, and it is often difficult for youth to distinguish where one ends and another beings.* They awaken lust and stir evil thoughts and sex desires. They are but parts of the whole family of related sins and indiscretions. . . . Too often, young people dismiss their petting with a shrug of their shoulders as a *little* indiscretion, while admitting that fornication is a base transgression. Too many of them are shocked, or feign to be, when told that what they have done in the name of petting *was in reality fornication.* (*The Miracle of Forgiveness*, pp. 65–66; emphasis added.)

Married people, in their expression of physical love, require a period of sexual arousal which includes rather intimate foreplay. Intimate touching and caressing are important dimensions of this sexual expression between a husband and his wife. Outside of the marriage covenant such intimate contact is off-limits, out-of-bounds, and sinful. Rather than stressing the negative, however, President David O. McKay portrayed the ideal:

> Marriage in the temple is one of the most beautiful things in all the world. . . . A young man looks, rightfully, upon that bride who will be the mother of his children as being as pure as a snowflake, as spotless as a sunbeam, as worthy of motherhood as any virgin. It is a glorious thing for a woman thus to wear the robes and be the pride of a young elder's heart, one who trusts her to be the head of his household.
>
> She trusts him as being as worthy of fatherhood as she is of motherhood, and rightfully, too, because on his shoulders are the robes of the Holy Priesthood, testifying to his young bride, and to all, of his worthiness.
>
> Together they stand in the house of the Lord to testify and covenant before him that they will be true to the covenants they make that day, each keeping himself or herself to the other and no one else. That is the highest ideal of marriage ever given to man. If those covenants are kept as sacred as sacred covenants should be kept, there would be fewer broken hearts among wives and fewer among the husbands. A covenant is a sacred thing. (*Improvement Era*, June 1969, pp. 28–29.)

Improving Sexual Intimacy in Marriage

It is appropriate, after reviewing some aspects of our theology regarding intimate relationships, to consider how married couples can enhance their ability to communicate and share what constitutes the most satisfying approach to sexual fulfillment.

First, couples, whether newly married or with years of experience, need to know that this relationship requires patience, understanding, and a desire to become educated in this aspect of marriage. It will require frequent monitoring. There must be a basic willingness to reveal one's own sexual preferences, feelings, and responses. Sexual intimacy is a new venture for brides and grooms, who are learning to cooperate, assist, and provide instruction to each other on a delicate subject. We must be good teachers and humble students. From the time we marry until the end of the life cycle, the complexities of our lives and certain physical changes that affect our sexual response may dictate some adjustments. Our sexual enjoyment may be different during pregnancy, following childbirth, or in our later years. Sexual interest is not static. Aging affects hormonal levels, and may make necessary more time for sexual arousal. But there is no reason why healthy individuals should not find satisfaction in their sexual relations for their entire lives.

Second, it is clear that sexual fulfillment begins with the quality of the marriage in the nonsexual areas. It is difficult for either spouse to give himself freely and fully to the spouse without fear of being rejected or hurt, if the companion is upset or angry. The sexual dimension is a barometer of the couple's total marriage experience. Dating and courting should be part of a lifelong process in which romantic adventures between companions are frequent and creative and therefore set the stage for heightened sexual pleasure and fulfillment.

Third, in general men probably have a greater sexual "drive" or interest (since orgasm is more predictable for them and therefore sexual release may be an important goal). If that is true in your marriage, it will require mutual understanding. The husband will need to exercise self-control, restraint, and charity in being sensitive to his companion's needs, desires, and interests. On the other hand, a wife may want to make herself more available for sexual relations, or initiate intimacy more frequently with her husband, because she understands that to him love and sex are so closely related. But charity must be the ruling virtue. Mutual consideration between spouses will allow each one to feel comfortable in initiating intimacy as well as realizing that there will be times when sexual relations are not appropriate or desirable to either one.

Knowing that husbands are sexually aroused by the erotic whereas women enjoy a romantic approach is important information. Of course, touching and holding, cuddling, and genuine expressions of love and endearment are important for both partners.

Fourth, both spouses should be aware that a number of factors may hinder their sexual satisfaction. If either one is unsympathetic to the pressures and worries of their companion, or when physical factors interfere—for example, weight, hygiene, and poor technique—these may detract from their responses. I remember counseling a rather large and heavy wife who was married to a very skinny husband. He was insensitive to basic hygiene, and she would fill the bathtub and physically undress him and haul him to the bathroom and bathe him before she could stand to be close to him.

Fifth, there will be times when neither spouse feels sexually aroused. Both will need to be mature enough to realize that there are no performance standards, no one to please except each other. Both must share their own honest feelings about sexual pleasure, realizing that charity and respect for the companion may override personal preferences at times.

Sixth, because of strong premarital sexual counsel and premarital abstinence, married couples may not be quite sure of how to be loving partners. Each must realize that the best source of help is the companion. The partner is the one that can best provide feedback on sexual technique. Sometimes we go for years without sharing with our partner information on our sexual preferences. A sincere desire to learn to please each other, coupled with a sense of humor—neither one embarrassing the other—can do much to increase sexual fulfillment. We must be as concerned about our spouse's sexual satisfaction as we are about our own. Both must be willing to assist in the arousal of their companion to sexual passion and expression.

Marriage is not just for sex, of course, but sex *is* a profound means of expressing love and commitment. It is designed to be a physical, emotional, and spiritual union; hence, it is a high form of validation. Just as a good marriage increases sexual ardor, so satisfactory sexual relations add soul-binding strength to the marriage. There are few ways as powerful as the sexual union of a man and woman to express affection and romantic love. By shutting out the world, a couple, in the intimacy and privacy of their own room, can renew their vows and pledge of fidelity. Feelings of love and appreciation—wanting to cooperate, to share in the joys of this life, to be therapeutic—are sown in the sacred union of a couple whose love is centered in charity and eternal covenants.

Both will be raised to a higher level of spirituality by acts of love which aptly express their emotional feelings. Every spirit child is entitled to the right to come into this world in the way that our Father has willed that souls should come—through parents who love each other and who want to rear their children in a home where love and affection abounds.

I have counseled couples who have gone years without sharing sexual intimacy. What a tremendous loss it has been to their souls! How consoling, how refreshing, how relaxing and wholesome physical intimacy should be for marrieds, who live in a world of stress and who are in need of frequent reassurance that their spouse loves and desires them.

When we meet each other's sexual needs, trust is strengthened and our ability to function as a team increases. We have a relationship that is intended to last forever. That means we can afford to be patient with our sexual feelings before marriage, and we can be patient with our sexual progress and the processes that will develop between us as partners. The media myth of the perfect (and instant) sexual fulfillment is just that—a myth. In many marriages it takes some time before we can establish the psychological and emotional closeness that is climaxed by the physical expression of love that should naturally follow between two people as their love matures and ripens. So much stress in our society is put on the mechanics, techniques, and skills of sex that it is easy to see a sexual encounter as an athletic performance. Well, it is not a game, and no one should be keeping score.

Another gentle reminder is that you're in this together. Neither partner has a problem alone. If the husband has some difficulty in sexual responses, that's a problem for both partners and not just for him. Similarly if the wife has a problem.

The sexual relationship is part of the total relationship. It cannot be separated from other facets of marital life. The husband who snarls his way home through five o'clock traffic, snaps when his wife asks, "How'd it go today?" and growls because dinner is tardy is not likely to find a warm reception when suddenly, at ten o'clock, he turns off the news and sends out amorous signals.

Here, then, are some of the tasks involved in establishing a pattern of healthy sexual intimacy.

1. *Acquire a vocabulary so that you can discuss intimacy comfortably.* We generally grow up not talking about anatomical realities, particularly with those of the opposite sex, and sometimes we simply lack the words. Even if we think we know the words, we sometimes feel embarrassed about using them. You may want to find a textbook that uses correct physiological terms for body parts and responses. Some may feel that this is too cold and unfeeling. My thinking is that those terms are infinitely preferable to

the kind of high-school talk you may have heard around your respective locker rooms, almost all of which connotes some kind of disrespect for either your own body or your partner's. Or, you may want to create your own glossary of terms.

2. *As you discover what pleases you and what you enjoy, tell your spouse.* It's your responsibility to assist your companion—after all, you know yourself best. You may wish that your partner could read your mind and your body; eventually, in a good sexual relationship you will be so in tune with each other that you may be able to do so. But that will probably come much later.

3. *Take some responsibility in explaining when you feel comfortable initiating love-making and when you want your partner to, and what an easy frequency is for you.* Some couples let the clock or the calendar decide when they're in the mood. And for some couples that's a system that works. However, if someone wants to change the "rules," then the relationship may not allow for it and spontaneity may become a casualty of bewilderment.

Some couples protest that actually having to ask makes the experience too "commercial"—like asking when it's time to see the dentist again. Also, isn't it devastating to have a direct request refused? What these couples don't realize is that they are using a code of signals that is just as clear and explicit as language but without a way of talking about the message. After all, if Joan puts on her lacy negligee and wanders into the living room brushing her hair and Allen looks up from the income taxes and mumbles, "Don't wait up," Joan *has* made a request and it *has* been refused. Her only choices now are to try to be understanding, or to feel hurt and undesirable. Wouldn't it be better for her to put her arms around his neck and whisper "I think I'd like to make love tonight if you feel like it," and for Allen to quickly change his mind about the priorities? (In fact, anyone who would not put off taxes for a little "therapy" may have other problems too.)

4. *Know what constitutes a good experience for your partner.* It means that you have to learn from your spouse about

moods, timing, and what is relaxing, stimulating, and pleasurable. Both of you should be able to answer these questions: What situations make love-making the best experience for me? for you? What is really needed and wanted in the way of techniques for me? for you? What aspects of love-making are the most pleasurable for me? for you? What about frequency? environment? And even if I know what the answers generally have been in these situations before, how about *this* time?

Phrases such as "I really enjoy it when you . . ." or "How do you feel about . . ." or "I think the thing I enjoy most about our intimacy is . . ." are questions or statements that are relevant for any married couple to share.

For "old marrieds," part of the process is realizing that a series of steps exist that lead from the first physical touch to the most passionate embrace. What are those steps in your marriage? Some couples tend to skip the preliminary steps after they have been married for a while and focus only on the final stages of sexual expression. Sometimes a reminder is warranted that those preliminary phases make the final steps not only possible but more satisfying. Often the greatest tenderness and romance are expressed either before or after the actual act of love.

Counselors see women who say: "The only time my husband ever tells me he loves me is when we are being intimate." Or, "I really dread the times when we can't have sex, because my husband is so hard to live with. He is angry, sullen, and irritable during those times." When a husband communicates (manipulates?) to his wife that her value and lovability depend on her sexual availability, it is difficult for her to feel that she is loved for herself and her contributions to the union, rather than simply for her body. Sex should be a part of love, not a substitute or equivalent for it. As I said earlier, patience with each other will be essential in this most intimate of marital experiences, the supreme expression of love to one another.

Counselors also deal with situations in which wives are rightfully resisting the invasion of their personhood that occurs when a husband insists that it is his "right" to enjoy marital relations and it is her "obligation" to cooperate—regardless of her personal wishes. Some men have equated this disguised selfishness as a part of their "presiding in the home." Although both partners must be sensitive about their motivations for intimacy—in initiating it, in cooperating in it, and in refusing it—President David O. McKay could not have been more explicit when he said, "A woman should be queen of her own body. The marriage covenant does not give the man the right to enslave her or to abuse her or to use her merely for the gratification of his passion." (*Gospel Ideals* [Salt Lake City: The Improvement Era, 1953], p. 471.)

A sensitive area is the question of propriety for married couples. The Church leaders have been clear that they have no wish to provide a list of either acceptable or unacceptable activities, but they have also been clear that certain standards ought to prevail. President Kimball, in denouncing "unwarranted tampering with or defilement of" the body, noted that "even in marriage there can be some excesses and distortions" (*Ensign*, May 1974, p. 7). President N. Eldon Tanner warned the priesthood of "evil and degrading practices which, in the world, are not only condoned but encouraged. Sometimes married couples in their intimate expression of love to one another are drawn into practices that are unholy, unworthy, and unnatural." (In Conference Report, Oct. 1978, pp. 60–61.)

As to that, the spiritual sensitivities of both partners ought surely to be observed and respected. If either one feels that the Spirit is grieved by a particular practice or they cannot agree to use it, wisdom would dictate that that activity be avoided.

A current challenge to some marriages is the threat of pornography. As Elder Marvin J. Ashton explained, exposure to obscenity results in "distorted views of personal conduct." A person who indulges in pornography "becomes unable to relate to others in a normal, healthy way." The partner then becomes an object rather than a companion and an eternal partner. Elder Ashton also noted pornography's addictive effect and its desensitizing results, an effect which counselors and therapists have traced on some of their clients. He made an eloquent appeal that Latter-day Saints refrain from such indulgence, because the Holy Ghost could not enlighten such a person. (In Conference Report, Oct. 1977, p. 108.) Elder David B. Haight was clear about the lack of control over the media and how important it is that we be selective in our television and movie viewing (see "Personal Morality," *Ensign*, Nov. 1984, pp. 70–73).

God intended that men and women enjoy their sexuality within appropriate bounds of mutual acceptability and spiritual sanction. Surveys among happily married people indicate that their sexual relations vary a great deal in frequency and type, but they all accept and enjoy creativity, variety, and spontaneity as part of this affirming relationship.

Elder Boyd K. Packer wrote:

> The greatest deception foisted upon the human race in our day is that overemphasis of physical gratification as it is related to romantic love. It is merely a repetition of the same delusion that has been impressed on every generation in ages past. When we learn that physical gratification is only incident to, and not the compelling force of love itself, we have made a supreme discovery. If only physical gratification should interest you, you need not be selective at all. This power is possessed by almost everyone. Alone, without attendant love, this relationship becomes nothing—indeed, less and worse than nothing. (*Eternal Love* [Salt Lake City: Deseret Book Company, 1973], p. 15.)

In conclusion, let it be said again that Latter-day Saints' sexual powers are God-given and are sanctioned within the framework of marriage. Perhaps in no other way in mortality do we so fully express our love and commitment to each other as in our intimate association. We thereby reaffirm our love and are reminded of our eternal covenants and promises as husband and wife. On the bases discussed in this chapter, sexual relations should be meaningful and should be enjoyed as frequently as is mutually agreeable within the bounds the Lord has set.

Family Relations 9

Tammy and Jeff had really looked forward to being parents. Their first two children seemed calm, happy, and easy to love. Though things were not perfect, they felt secure in their parenting skills and they decided that another baby would be a good idea. Enter little Josh into the picture.

For five months Josh seemed lovable and quiet, but then something happened. At ten months he was trying to climb out of his crib and succeeding. He raged when things did not go just the way he wanted them. There was no place in the house he could not get to. Tammy paddled him when he got into trouble and put him in his crib to keep him out of trouble and out of her hair for a few minutes. In sixty seconds he would be out dumping over plants, knocking all the books off the bookshelves, and pulling his dad's tapes out of their container. Tammy would drag him screaming and kicking back to his room, and the contest would begin anew.

One day Tammy became so frustrated with trying to control him that she tied his bedroom doorknob to the bathroom doorknob across the hall so that he couldn't get out of his room, at least for a while. He screamed and kicked and at last fell asleep in a heap on the floor. When Jeff came home from work that evening and saw the tied doorknobs (Tammy had used his tie), he couldn't believe that she would stoop so low. Imagine letting a one-year-old get to you like that!

That evening Tammy left the children with Jeff while she attended a class. When she returned, the house was a disaster, every room strewn with toys and mess, and Jeff lay collapsed on the living room floor. In the hall she could see Josh's bedroom door tied to the bathroom door once again. She had to laugh. "Imagine not being able to control a one-year-old," she teased.

But it wasn't really funny. Getting up at two in the morning to find eighteen-month-old Josh making lemonade on the kitchen counter in the dark or watching him climb up the door frames and hang upside down from their tops, or having him scream and pummel her with his fists until she had bruises, made her feel as if she were losing control, as if she were not at all sure that she was cut out to raise this child. She had spanked him so many times that she worried that sometime she might hurt him when she lost her temper.

She talked with her husband, read every available book on child rearing, and spent a good deal of time praying about her problem. When he had just turned three she attended a class about disciplining children given at a Women's Conference at Brigham Young University. The instructor had no other credentials than the fact that she had mothered seven children. As Tammy listened to her theories and methods, she knew that what she was hearing was an answer to her prayers. She was afraid that Josh might be a little too young to understand the method, but at least she had some concrete ideas to try with him. After almost three years of feeling out of control and desperate, she was able to regain control of her child and her life.

Tammy never stopped loving Josh, but there were certainly times when she stopped liking him. Yet even through the worst times she knew that Heavenly Father had given him to her to raise, and He must have felt some confidence in her abilities. After a time she realized that if she prayed for help the Lord would not just make things better but he would give her the strength and discernment to search out and recognize true and helpful principles and methods of working with Josh.

We are told over and over again the incredible value of the souls that are being born to this earth right now. Even though it is sometimes hard to look at our children and see their greatness, we must struggle every day they are in our homes to help them reach their potential. We don't know what they will have to deal with in their lives, but we can be fairly certain that it will not all be easy. They are going to need all the help they can get from us, their parents. They will be the ones to help keep our families strong, our Church prosperous and righteous, and our nation healthy.

Parents must be keenly aware of their responsibility, the commitment, and the challenge to provide an environment in which these spirits may grow and learn of their mission and then go forth to serve others. The prophets have been consistent in their counsel that parents use the Sabbath day and Monday evenings, at least, as times to instruct their children in gospel principles and to share activities that will strengthen family ties. There is a great need for little ones to grow up full of faith and to be knowledgeable concerning the mission of the Lord and the Church in this dispensation. Parents must set as a high priority sharing this information with their offspring.

I see three areas where parents can gain strength in rearing valiant, moral children. They are (1) using the gift of the Holy Ghost to be a more effective spouse and parent; (2) parenting as partners; and (3) using the children as a source of help to strengthen the entire family. Suggested ways to develop strengths in these areas follow.

Individual Revelation for Personal Stewardships

As frustrated as Tammy became with Josh, she never

felt that she could give up. She knew that he was valuable property—a child of our Father in Heaven. It is pretty sobering to realize, as I've stressed before, that Heavenly Father trusts us to raise his own offspring. We accept the responsibility for rearing these children.

I think there are many who cruise through their family living without stopping to evaluate their progress realistically and fairly. Perhaps they do not want to know how they are doing. Sometimes knowing that we are not giving all that we should is uncomfortable. Nevertheless, it is something which we must all do if we expect to progress and improve. It may be easier if we start with the knowledge that we are not going to get it all right from the start. In fact, we are probably never going to get it all right. But we can move closer to that goal. And we must know that our Father in Heaven wants us to succeed. He has not left us without help. He has given us the gift of the Holy Ghost, a member of the Godhead, to inspire and instruct us so that we can succeed in our own life and effectively rear each individual spirit child that he assigns to us. As parents, we have the right to receive inspiration from the Spirit of the Lord in our callings. He will nurture us and lead us to develop the attributes of Christ—an important reason for our coming to earth.

When we are teachable and humble, when we truly desire to improve ourselves, then we may begin asking questions of ourselves with the desire to do better. We also have a prayer in our heart to the Lord for help. "Heavenly Father, I am grateful to live on the earth in this final dispensation. Please help me as a father and husband to see ways for me to improve my own life and spirituality, to be of greater service to thee." In doing this, we must avoid the "Oliver Cowdery" syndrome. Recall that Oliver was chastized by the Lord because he failed to "do his homework." He thought the Lord would do all the work for him if he merely asked. "But, behold, I say unto you, that you must study it out in your mind; then you must ask me if it be right," was the Lord's answer (D&C 9:8). If we do not use our own minds and hearts while pleading for the Lord's assistance, we may be guilty of the same fault.

Here's a technique I use. To review my performance in my family stewardship, I place the names of each family member on a sheet of paper and look carefully at the relationship I have with each member. (Ages are given simply for illustration.)

My Family

Geri—wife

David—teenage son	Jonathan—12
Terri—teenage daughter	Andy—10
Becky—teenage daugther	Mandy—7

Beginning with my wife, Geri, I need to ask myself some penetrating questions about my performance. How does she view me as a husband? When was the last time I invited her to get away for a break? When was the last time we really had a good chat about our family and personal goals? Does she enjoy my company? Do I allow her to be herself? Am I too dominating? possessive? irritable? critical? What am I doing to lighten her load with the children and her work at home? What kind of leadership am I providing in our family? Do I listen to her ideas and take counsel from her? Does she feel secure as my wife and partner? Do I help her enjoy her talents? Do I show her enough nonsexual affection and love? Do I share my thoughts and feelings freely with her? Is our intimacy meaningful to her?

The questions can be many and varied. The important thing is that I ponder what makes a strong marriage relationship and then think of specific ways in which I can improve in my personal performance as a husband.

After I have reviewed the relationship with my sweetheart, each child deserves a similar process. Let me illustrate with David. First, prayer: "Oh, Father, I am so grateful for Dave. I pray that I might be a good father with him, that I might rear him as thou wilt have me do. Help me now to think of ways to strengthen our relationship. I love him so." Here are some questions that I might ask myself: "When was the last time Dave and I had a good father-son talk about girls? love? feelings? schooling? life? Does he come to me with his problems and concerns? only for money or the car? or not at all? Why? Why not? Is he well prepared and anxious to serve a mission? What can I do to draw him closer to me? Have I helped him to mature spiritually? Is he sure of my love?"

I may need to make some specific plans to be with him and express my love to him. Maybe breakfast out—just the two of us—working together on a project, taking time for some good discussions alone, or quiet talks at bedtime. The principle is to ask yourself some basic questions about this relationship and make some plans to improve as a parent.

If you do this with each child, making an action plan for the coming days, you will find that the Lord, after you have done your part, will inspire you in your parental responsibilities in specific ways. This review also insures that you don't neglect any of your children and that your influence will be constant in their lives.

To succeed in our personal stewardships, we must review them occasionally to make sure that we are making progress, not in a spirit of panic, nor in running faster than we have strength (see D&C 10:4), but in competently thrusting in the sickle.

Parenting as Partners

Parents who work as partners will be stronger than those who don't. Husbands often feel they are too busy with their work to really share the privilege of rearing the children. They feel their jobs are independent from what goes on in the home. Nothing could be further from the truth. From the first day of life, fathers are important in the lives of their children. Husbands and wives need to work together to help each child progress. As a husband, I learned long ago that my wife spends more physical time with the children and is therefore more aware of what is going on in their lives. Therefore I need to counsel with her about each of the children. We need mutual input. We need to discuss each child's personality, health, and developmental stage, and determine how best to assist him or her. Here are some concrete examples.

Child's Name	Strengths	Weaknesses	Plans and Goals
Billy (12)	Good mind, obedient, outgoing, does well in school	Sarcastic, careless with possessions, teases others	Family home evening lesson on loving others and taking care of our things
Mike (10)	Affectionate, sensitive, likes animals	Forgets rules, rebellious at times	Express love to him often, find a puppy or kitten, review family rules and reasons for them

Reviewing each child's strengths and weaknesses, as partners, brings some focus on where help and strength is needed with a particular child. A team effort lifts the burden from just one spouse having to make decisions alone. The responsibilities of parenthood ought to be shared. That was the Lord's intent. The children will benefit from a united front and consistency on the part of parents who feel love and support from each other and show it.

The Children as a Source of Feedback

Feedback from the children themselves is a third excellent source for helping parents. Since our children are the objects of our parenting efforts, they know better than anyone else how well we are doing in our tasks. The purpose of family home evenings and family councils is to teach, to seek feedback on our successes and our failures, and to learn ways that we can live in greater harmony. We desire gentle feedback and helpful ways to improve as fathers and mothers and as a total family. Children look forward to an opportunity to comment, to share their insights about the dynamics of the family's interactions—if you will encourage them. (You must be very gentle about it and not react negatively to their genuine reflections.) Try some of the following topics—assuming they are old enough to share their insights.

1. *Your marriage.* "How do you children view Mom and me as a married couple?" (If one has trouble understanding your intention, elaborate.) "Do you see us as a very warm, affectionate, loving couple, or do you see us angry with each other?" "Does it seem to you that we argue and quarrel a lot, or do you think we really love each other?" You will be surprised to learn what insights your children have to offer from observing the two of you. Listen carefully to their perceptions.

2. *Your discipline methods.* "How do you kids feel about the way Mom and I discipline you? Are we too strict, or do you think we are too easygoing?" Your children will have views about this since they are the objects of your discipline methods. What are their genuine reactions to your efforts to control or correct them? See if they have memories of your spanking them when they were little. How did they feel about it at the time? How do they feel now? How will they discipline their own children?

3. *Your family as a family.* "Do you think we work well together as a family, or do we argue and grumble and get unpleasant with each other? What do you think we can do to improve our relationships with each other?"

4. *Managing money in our home.* "Do you like the way we spend money? Do you think we are tightwads, or do we throw money around? How is our allowance system working? Any suggestions for improvement?"

5. *Television rules.* "How do you like the rules we have about watching TV? Are we too strict or too lenient? Have you seen any shows that embarrassed you? How would you like us to handle watching TV in our home?"

6. *Church.* "How do you children feel about attending church? Sometimes kids become inactive because they feel that their parents shoved the gospel down their throats. Do you feel we are doing that, or do you enjoy going? Would you go if we were not here to encourage you?"

7. *Work schedules around the house.* "How do you feel about the way we assign jobs? Could we do it better? What changes would you suggest? Is there a better way for us to assign out jobs in our family?"

8. *Career interests.* "What kind of professions or jobs interest you? Do you think Dad has a good job? (or Mother?) What kind of career would you girls like?"

9. *Improving our family relations.* "What can we do to make life better at home? What one thing do you think we could do to make our home happier?" (Give each an opportunity to respond.)

10. *Quality of family home evenings.* "How do you feel about our family home evenings? Do I talk and lecture too much? Should we rotate the lessons more? Which family home evenings have you enjoyed the most?"

Your family ought to be a problem-solving unit. Your job, as parents, is to develop a healthy communication system and an environment for discussing any problem or concern that arises in your family so that you can reach acceptable solutions. You may decide issues as a group, or you may need to go one-on-one. The most important thing is that you let family members know that you care how they feel, that you dare to open up and venture away from the "safe" topics—reading scriptures and telling or reading stories—into deeper topics that are relevant to your family, the "nitty-gritties." We really don't have our children in our home very long. We need to insure that while they are there we are teaching and instructing and blessing them—consistently and positively.

In addition to counseling with (1) the Lord, (2) your spouse, and (3) your children, there are two other principles of parenting that may be helpful. They include family traditions and child tracking.

Family Traditions

What will your children remember about their early years in your family? (Believe it or not, they will be gone someday!) Will their memories of your family life be fun?

inspirational? positive? Or will your children be somewhat anxious to leave and get away from your home? One of the things that happy families seem to have in common are family traditions which they have developed over the years. Here are a number of traditions that might have some value for you to adopt or add to your own repertoire. Remember that a family tradition, established by repeating activities you enjoy, should bring unity, love, harmony, cooperation, and spiritual growth to your family.

1. *Reading or telling stories to children at bedtime.* This is a very important practice. Not only does it help children learn to be interested in reading (consequently they will be more successful in school), but it sets a pattern for parents to visit with them at night so that long after you have stopped reading to them (or vice versa) they are comfortable in having you visit with them at bedtime. Teenagers, to whom you want to stay close, will be more accessible when you have been consistent in your nightly visits.

2. *Spending one-on-one time with each child regularly.* You need to have special things you do with each child and he needs to feel you are aware of his individual concerns and feelings about events in his life. It should be special to be alone with Mom or Dad and feel loved by them. Take a different one with you when you go shopping, for a hamburger, on an errand, or even to your place of employment.

3. *Inviting a single parent and children, or needy family over for dinner or family activity.* Sharing your own blessings with others reminds the children of the need to be charitable to others and to experience the joy that comes from giving of self. There are many singles and widow(er)s that need some friendship and an association with children.

4. *Regular family trips and vacations.* Children look back on their early lives and remember the fun of being together on trips as a family. Set aside some of your income for recreation and leisure time together. Then relax and have a good time. Some families go on trips that are tense and unhappy for everyone. Potentially great vacations have been ruined by temper and impatience.

5. *Favorite travel and car games.* Make your travel time together fun with games and pretrip planning. Alphabet games using signs along the road, guessing how far it is to the next overpass or landmark using the odometer, and similar games are good time- and mile-passers.

6. *Pumpkin carving or painting on Halloween.* This is a time for kids and families to capitalize on the opportunities to work together to decorate the house and yard. Dad can take the little ones out to "trick or treat." Remind them to express thanks to those who treat them.

7. *Christmas caroling, choosing a Christmas tree as a family, decorations, and the Christmas story.* Of all the times when traditions are easy to begin and so meaningful to the family, Christmas is the most obvious holiday to enjoy one another. However, in many families Christmas is a time of tension because of money, in-laws, parties, more time together, and children out of school. Christmas can be a strain on families, as every marriage counselor can attest.

8. *Celebrating and recognizing national holidays.* Patriotism is not outmoded, and our children should know that we love and support our government and leaders. We can put our flags out on appropriate days, say the pledge of allegiance together, and share other similar activities.

9. *Encouraging scripture reading and family journals.* Why not purchase for your children copies of the new scriptures for their very own use? Bibles and triple combinations are now available at very nominal cost. We ought to replace our old ones and furnish the children theirs at birthdays or special events. When presenting them to the children be sure that both of you write a personal note in the flyleaf.

10. *Family home evenings and family councils.* Of all the traditions you initiate, don't forget this one. You will have many decisions to make over the years and many topics to discuss with the children. Make these times enjoyable so that your family looks forward to getting together for discussions.

11. *Family reunions—small and large.* Encourage family ties with grandparents, uncles and aunts, and cousins.

"Blood is thicker than water" will always hold true. Our children need to know of their heritage and be acquainted with their immediate relatives.

12. *Making family crests, flags, mottos, or yells.* What do you do to unify your family, to encourage family pride, or to gather your family when they are scattered in a park? A family banner or flag or crest might help or a call that is unique to your tribe. Some families have special whistles or signals to call all of them together for an important message or to head home.

13. *Carrying a penny taped in your shoe to remind you of family goals and the importance of being a member of your family.* Give the children a new penny to put in one of their shoes (inside heel) so that when they put their shoes on each day they are reminded of their responsibility to represent your family, church, or country, to the best of their ability that day!

14. *Special recognitions: best room, talk in church, most helpful during the week, and so forth.* Reward with double allowance, special place settings at mealtime, or similar private or family recognition.

15. *Family prayer.* This is crucial. Let your children know that family prayer is an important priority in their young lives, a habit that should be lifelong. Even when you all arrive home late or other distractions arise, make this an important tradition in your home.

16. *Church attendance.* Perhaps this is not usually viewed as a tradition, but it should be one of the most obvious ones. Church is not for our benefit only, but to give service to others and to fellowship with the Saints.

17. *Blessings before the beginning of a school year, summer camp, and other major events.* This tradition is especially important in making the jump to new schools or moving from elementary to junior high (middle school) or on to high school and college.

18. *Book reading and reading marathons.* We ought to encourage children to read good books and literature and even the daily paper. Children should come to know the

classics. Too often time is wasted on questionable television programs when good literature goes begging.

19. *Parlor games.* There are many family games that can bring unity and recreation. Be sure to use them to build solidarity and not as competition where bad feelings and name-calling ensue. Don't be as concerned about winning as you are about having a good time. Uno, Trivial Pursuit, Monopoly, chess, checkers, Rook, and many gospel games are now available to families. Games in the yard —such as "kick the can" and "hide and seek"—are also fun.

20. *Watching television programs together.* There are more and more classic television movies and documentaries about historical events that can be an excellent source of family entertainment. Carefully review the television guides available to you and plan your viewing.

21. *Family work and service projects—gardening, crafts, family programs, and talent development.* All are helpful to family unity.

22. *Homey, wholesome, and happy memory-builders.* Breakfast out on a child's birthday is always a fun time for children. Special poems, songs, music, and talents can brighten a family's time together.

23. *Family greetings when a member has been away.* It is fun to welcome one of the family back home after being away to the mission field, college, camp, or just about anywhere. It is a good feeling to know that you were missed.

Add these to your own list.

Child Tracking

There are times when we may want to "track" our parenting efforts over a period of time to check our progress with our children. Table 9.1 allows that to be done for a week at a time. At the top of the page place the name of one of your children whom you would like to observe for a week. At the end of each day write down the

Table 9.1

CHILD TRACKING
HOW WELL AM I PARENTING?

Name of child to monitor: _____

Activities with this child today:	MON	TUE	WED	THU	FRI	SAT	SUN	Weekly Total (+, −)
1. Verbally expressed praise or compliments								
2. Read a story together								
3. Prayed together								
4. Hugged, wrestled, or touched lovingly								
5. Worked together on a task								
6. Listened patiently to his concerns								
7. Greeted with enthusiasm—home from school								
8. Played a game together								
9. Discussed a rule or principle								
10. Spent time together playing								
11. Took on an errand or task								
12. (Other)								
1. Hit or slapped, shoved, or yanked								
2. Spanked with hand, object								
3. Punished (quiet time, grounding, etc.)								
4. Criticized, sarcastic, or belittling								
5. Interrupted, moralized, lectured								
6. Judged behavior and actions harshly								
7. Embarrassed in front of friends								
8. Labeled with unkind terms								
9. Swore at child								
10. No contact at all with child								
11. (Other)								

Grand total of pluses _____

Grand total of minuses _____

Instructions: Record at the end of each day the number of times you did each or any of the activities. At the end of the week total the number of times you performed each activity with this child. Total the pluses and minuses for the week. Evaluate with your spouse your relationship with this child and determine what improvements you both can make.

number of times you did any of the activities listed with that child. At the end of the week add the number of times each activity occurred. At the same time decide which ones are positive or negative and total the pluses and minuses for the week. At the end of that time you should be able to see what influence—positive or negative—you are having on the child. (If you use the sheet for three weeks it will train you to be a good parent because you will learn the activities that will increase the likelihood of good things happening between you and this child.)

Effective Fathering   *10*

Tom was good at making money—in fact, he was great at it. Tom made sure that his wife and children had every toy and convenience that was available. He took them on lavish vacations and made sure they ate at the best places. He worked hard at his profession, and when he was home he worked hard to keep the garden and the yard in tip-top shape and all the things in the house running smoothly. But his rare moments of relaxation were spent in front of the TV. He felt awkward with his children and had little to say to them unless they wanted to work with him side by side in the garden. Even then, he became easily frustrated with their inability to do things right. When they were small, he said that he didn't know what to say to them, and he would talk to them when they were older. When they were older, they didn't particularly want to talk to him. And he couldn't understand what had gone wrong—after all, hadn't he always given them everything they had needed and wanted?

He had given them everything—everything except what they really needed. Unfortunately, it is a common experience in counseling interviews to find that fathers are often negligent and somewhat insensitive to the needs of their family members. It is often easier for them to give their money and advice than their time and interest. They often struggle to know how to lead out as the family head. The purpose of this chapter is to help fathers understand the greatness of their callings and to present some practical ways for them to improve their performance. The following ideas can help fathers enrich the lives of their family members.

1. *Leadership.* Some fathers misunderstand their role as "head of the home" and consider themselves the primary decision-maker. Anyone questioning his decision is immediately reprimanded.

In one family I dealt with, a Cub Scout–aged boy had earned seventeen dollars working on a project. He kept the cash in one-dollar bills which he flashed all over the neighborhood and schoolground. His mother had warned him repeatedly during the week to put the money away for safe-keeping, but the warning went unheeded. On the following Sunday morning, David came into his parents' bedroom crying because he was missing two of the dollars. Exasperated, Susan replied, "Don't cry to me about it. I have warned you all week to put it away in a safe place!"

As he continued to cry, Paul, the father, got up and took two one-dollar bills out of his wallet and handed them to David. Upset, Susan told Paul how she had been warning David all week about the possibility of losing his money. Paul shrugged, "Well, what's a couple of dollars. He'll be happy again."

Susan explained the situation in greater detail, concerned that he did not grasp the importance of this teaching moment for the son. When she had finished her second explanation, Paul responded, "Have you forgotten the covenant you made when we were married?"

Of course, this man was remembering only part of the story. The Lord has instructed:

> No power or influence can or ought to be maintained by virtue of the priesthood, only by persuasion [reasoning, discussion, talking, counseling together], by long-suffering [not emotional outbursts, put-downs, or sarcasm], by gentleness and meekness [especially with a wife and children], and by love unfeigned [unconditional];
>
> By kindness, and pure knowledge [obtained from reading the scriptures and good books, praying, counseling with your wife who knows your children intimately], which shall greatly enlarge the soul [your soul as well as theirs] without hypocrisy [saying one thing and doing another], and without guile. (D&C 121:41–42.)

A father has a powerful incentive to be full of charity, to rise to his tallest spiritual stature, to manifest love and compassion when he understands the important stewardship the Lord has given him as the priesthood holder and leader over some of His choicest spirits. This does not mean, however, that we are to be permissive and allow the children to dictate the course the family pursues. We need to develop a keen balance between control and freedom. Children need limits and rules. As they mature, develop competence and earn more of our trust, we gradually grant them more and more freedoms. We must instruct them in their responsibilities, seek their compliance to reasonable rules of conduct, and be charitable in our treatment of offenses. Where the rules of the family are violated, the Lord counsels: "Reproving betimes [immediately thereafter] with sharpness, when moved upon by the Holy Ghost; and then showing forth afterwards an increase of love toward him whom thou hast reproved, lest he esteem thee to be his enemy;

That he may know that thy faithfulness is stronger than the cords of death." (D&C 121:43–44.)

However, in order to discipline children effectively, you must first establish a relationship with them. Discipline without love often leads to rebellion. Parental values and teachings will be accepted much more readily if they are preceded by a genuine effort to extend love and charity to each child.

When you are home, Dad, it is your opportunity to be closely involved in the family activities. There are times when you may want to call the family together, counsel with them, instruct them, review family rules, initiate family prayer, or provide leadership and encouragement. That doesn't mean that you have to be the originator of every idea, but that you (1) counsel with your wife about family matters, (2) call your family together for important announcements or instructions, and (3) present any problems or concerns to the family for their input.

When everyone has had his say, you may summarize for the family what appears to you to be the best solution. "Why don't we leave for church at 12:30 in the station wagon. We'll have our family prayer at 12:20. I'd like us all to bring our scriptures to church today and let's shock the teachers." Or "Monday evening for family night we are going to the park for a picnic and some kickball. Mom and I were thinking we could go about 6:00 P.M. Robert, is that a good time for you? Janet? Wally? Okay, let's plan to leave then."

The children need to see you, Dad, announcing and initiating family councils, get-togethers, rap sessions, and presenting matters that affect the entire family. It indicates that you are involved, that you care.

2. *Take time to visit with and come to know your children intimately.* Dad, since you are gone much of the day away from the home, it is crucial that you take the time to visit with your children, to understand their motivations, their very "heartbeat." When you are home, you need to *be* home. Let your children know *your* heart too, and they will be more secure in your love and concern for their welfare. This happens most easily when you take time to be with them on a one-on-one basis. Visit with them and listen to their concerns and feelings. Review with them their school experiences; their feelings about the Church and the

gospel, their friends; your home; your love for their mom; brothers and sisters; and your frustrations and successes. The more you know your children, the better your family prayers will be, because you will offer practical prayers in their behalf. For example, "Heavenly Father, please help Terri in her chemistry test today. She has studied long and hard to learn the material. She needs thy Spirit to be with her today." You need to know your children and their schedules well enough to plead for their welfare.

Take time to go over their schoolwork and compositions, look at their drawings, and find out from their teachers (school and Church) how they behave in class, what their instructors see as their strengths and weaknesses. Attend their performances, music or dance recitals, and be unreserved in your approval of their efforts and success.

Bishop H. Burke Peterson expressed concern in 1977 about "the growing number of homes in the Church where the influence of a father is hardly felt." Although he listed divorce as one of the three reasons for this situation, the other two causes were aimed directly at fathers who still, at least on paper, headed their family: "pursuit of wealth and indifference to sacred things." He stressed, "In this life a father is never released from his responsibility. . . . A father's calling is an eternal calling if he lives worthily." ("The Father's Duty to Foster the Welfare of His Family," *Ensign*, Nov. 1977, p. 87.) In contrast, by stressing that bishops and stake presidents are called, serve, and then released, I suspect that Bishop Peterson was subtly making the point that some devoted Church leaders tend to put their families second, after their service in the kingdom, and thus may be postponing their responsibilities as fathers—hoping that their children will still be there when they are released.

To help you as a father to build good relationships with each of your children, you may want to try this idea. Purchase a box of large, empty gelatin pill capsules from a pharmacy. From the following list of activities pick out some that appeal to you and add some of your own. Write the ones you choose on a small piece of colored paper (a different color for the younger and the older children if you have a large family). Place the pills in a jar for your children to draw from on family home evening, or at a convenient time. You will have the entire week to carry out that activity with one of your children. Here are some ideas for these activities.

Younger Children

Let's go get an ice cream cone—you pick the flavor!

You have Daddy for one hour to do anything you want.

Let's just you and I play any game you would like to play.

This love note entitles you to a movie with Daddy as your date.

You pick a favorite story and Daddy will read with you.

You and I have a date with ''Ronald McDonald.''

Let's go to the park together to swing and feed the ducks or the pigeons.

This note is good for a wrestling match with Dad, or for a piggy-back ride.

Let's go to the library and check out some books to read.

This note is good for a treat at the day-old bread store.

This note allows you to go with me on my next business trip.

Let's make some cookies and surprise the family.

Let's make breakfast for the rest of the family.

Let's take the bus on a trip around town. We'll stop at some fun places.

This note is good for a bike ride together. We'll take along some picnic food.

This note can be redeemed for a new pen or pencil.

This note is good for a surprise from me sometime this week.

This note can be exchanged for me doing your jobs one day this week.

This note is good for a massage anytime you like.

Let's play catch together!

Let's surprise someone in our neighborhood or ward with a little service project or gift.

Let's write a thank-you letter to your teacher this week.

How about a hot fudge sundae or banana split—you pick.

Let's go for a hike together and learn something about nature.

Let's go play miniature golf.

How about a roller-skating hour together!

How about going to work with me for a day to be together. I'll show you what I do all day.

Older Children (over 12)

You will have breakfast in bed one day this week.

You pick the place and we'll go together.

Let's go bowling this week.

This love note entitles you to a night out with Dad to do anything you want.

Let's hit the Deseret Industries (or thrift store) to see what we can find for the family.

Let's share a couple of hours any way you like— talking, playing a game, homework—you choose.

How about some tennis (golf, basketball, etc.)!

I will bring a surprise home this week for you.

Let's get away for a shake or snack together this week.

Let's work on the yard together and get it shaped up. Afterwards we'll get a snack together.

Why don't we challenge the neighbors to a football (basketball) game on our lawn? (Or, you and me against your friends.)

Why don't we surprise one of the single parents in our ward with a night off while we babysit the children?

This is good for at least 5 ping-pong games. If I lose, we go to dinner.

This note is good for a driving lesson in the car.

This love note can be exchanged for my taking your paper route for one day (or your Saturday job).

This note can be redeemed for a new shirt (or blouse).

Let's cook dinner for the family one night this week.

Let's go drive some golf balls.

This note is good for a new cassette of great music.

How about going to the park and practicing your hitting and catching fly balls?

Where's the frisbee? Let's hit the park!

Let's take the whole family out to dinner this week.

How about the water slide (or, if winter, the tubing run)!

Let's do a service project for one of the ward members.

Let's make something fun in the shop, or repair something that needs to be fixed (work on the car together, explain how something works, etc.).

Let's go to the range and shoot the .22 rifle.

Be sure that while you are alone with the child you take time to talk to him, to listen to his ideas, to better understand his nature and disposition, and to express your love and approval. Coming to know each child as an individual and learning to appreciate his great potential will be one of the great experiences of your life.

3. *Be generous in your expressions of praise, positives, love, and affection.* I have a friend who spent her childhood winning awards, being a cheerleader and a student body officer in her school, earning top grades, and, when she finished high school, winning several scholarships to college. The harder she tried, the less her parents said about her accomplishments. It was as if they expected her to do all these things and never became involved or excited about what she had accomplished. As an adult, she feels as if she has spent her life trying to please other people and has never felt that she was loved enough.

Men sometimes feel that displays of tenderness and affection are unmanly and unnecessary, but these macho ideas have no place in a family. Children need desperately to know that they are loved, not just by what dad can buy them, but by both verbal expressions of love and nonverbal messages. Among the real tragedies of life are the great number of wives and children who are starving for a little praise and recognition from their husbands and fathers.

Though it is often hard to be positive with teenagers, they are at an age when positive feelings are needed most. Be sure to express your pride in them. "Dave, I am proud of you and your work at school (around the home, yard, farm, quorum, blessing the sacrament, etc.). I want you to know that I love you very much." Touch your children kindly, gently, and frequently. A good friend once told me that his most important priesthood assignment is to wrestle with his children. At times you may need to take on the whole bunch in a tussle. (Be gentle with them, for the time will come when you will want them to be gentle with you!) Don't be ashamed to hug your children, to express frankly and openly your love for them. If this is difficult for you, practice in private until it becomes easy and natural for you. It will.

4. *Control your temper.* It is hard for adults to understand sometimes how frightening an adult's temper outburst can be to a child. Months of good fathering efforts can be undone with emotional outbursts. Small children are frightened when they see their father (or mother) unable to control their emotions. We must be gentle and careful with children. The Savior counseled, "Suffer little children, and forbid them not, to come unto me: for of such is the kingdom of heaven" (Matthew 19:14).

As a priesthood holder you must remember President David O. McKay's counsel:

> No member of this Church, no husband or father, has the right to utter an oath in his home, or ever to express a cross word to his wife or to his children. By your ordination and your responsibility you cannot do it as a man who holds the priesthood and be true to the spirit within you. . . . You do what you can to produce peace and harmony, no matter what you may suffer. (*Improvement Era*, June 1969, p. 116.)

Elder ElRay L. Christiansen underscored the same theme:

> Someone has said, "The size of a man may be measured by the size of the things that make him angry." How true that is! To become upset and infuriated over trivial matters gives evidence of childishness and immaturity in a person. . . .
>
> Anger against *things* is senseless indeed!
>
> Because a wrench slips and we bruise our hand is no reason for throwing the wrench halfway across a wheat field. Having a flat tire on a busy downtown street will not be remedied by a tirade of words.
>
> Anger against *things* is bad enough, but when it is directed against people and it flares up with white-hot fury and caustic words, we have the makings of tragedy! . . .
>
> The man [or woman] with an uncontrolled temper is like an undisciplined child—he expresses his emotions explosively or by sulking, and disregards the feelings of those

about him. In the home, anger should be controlled and love should abound. . . .

. . . To lose our temper, to explode, to become ugly, punitive, and hateful when faced with frustrations is inexcusable. (*Ensign*, June 1971, pp. 37–38.)

The great penalty paid for temper outbursts (in addition to the possibility of physical abuse and injury) is that children will not come to you to risk personal concerns or to seek counsel. Do *you* confide in those who put you down? If you have been angry at your own children often, especially if they don't think they deserve the anger, it will be very difficult to build close, loving relationships.

We must remember that children are young, they are learning, as we once learned, and they are going to make mistakes. Let's give them some freedom to err, and teach them more effective ways in a controlled, loving, charitable environment.

5. *Teach children specific lessons.* Lisa's mother-in-law told her proudly, ''I never worried about you as long as Ron was with you. I knew that he respected you and wouldn't let anything happen that shouldn't. I trusted him completely.'' But she didn't bother to instruct Ron just what his responsibilities in a dating situation were. What she didn't realize was that Ron, taught only by the sexual escapades of an older brother, put constant sexual pressure on Lisa. Lisa *was* a good girl, and Ron loved her, and together they weathered the storm of their early dating years and are now happily married, but Lisa still resents the attitude of her in-laws that left the responsibility for their son's behavior on her shoulders.

Prophets have repeatedly warned us that we cannot shift to any other agency or person the responsibility to teach our children. Parents need to deal directly with the issues and standards that they want their children to model. Some of the most important ideals we want our children to learn are difficult to teach through modeling; they require some explanation and application through an understanding of basic principles. Learning how to handle death, for example, requires some explanation and help by parents. In table 10.1 I have compiled a list of topics that I feel every father and mother should teach their children. Look first at the entire list, then read through the thoughts I have expressed below on some of the mini-lessons.

Comments Related to Table 10.1

(1) *Education and vocational goals.* Students often come to college without much of an idea of what they want to study and make of their lives. From the time they are small, parents can awaken children to the demands and rewards of various means of earning a living. Father, take your children to work with you sometimes so that they can see what you do for a living. (Try to look busy while they are there.) Explain what you do to earn an income. Pressuring children into a specific type of vocation is certainly unwise, but parents have a responsibility to encourage their children to make good use of their educational pursuits.

(2) *Learning to work well.* A mission president said to me that his best missionaries were the "athletes and the farm boys." Can you guess why? How *do* you teach your children to work—particularly if they grow up in the city environment where opportunities to work are limited? What are you doing to help your children learn the value of work as therapy and to increase their value to a prospective employer? That is an important challenge.

(3) *Music appreciation.* What do your children know about good music, notes, rhythm? What kind of music do you play and encourage around your home? Do you ever take your children to concerts and cultural events so that they learn to listen to good music? Every child should have some background in this area—whether instrumental, vocal, or dance.

(4) *Unselfishness.* What are you doing as a father to insure that your children are not self-centered? egocentric? How do you go about helping your children to realize that

Table 10.1

WHAT VALUES ARE OUR CHILDREN LEARNING?

Attitudes and values concerning:	How Important Is It to Learn These Values?			Best Place to Teach These Values?				Extent to Which We Are Teaching These Values?		
	Very	Somewhat	Unimportant	School	Home	Church	TV	Often	Somewhat	Very little
1. Education and vocational goals										
2. Learning to work hard										
3. Music appreciation										
4. Unselfishness										
5. Responsibility-accountability										
6. Organization of time										
7. Reading good books										
8. Finishing a job										
9. Manners										
10. Morals, affection, love										
11. Money management										
12. Expressing gratitude										
13. Sportsmanship										
14. Apologizing										
15. Patience, meekness, kindness										
16. Communication skills										
17. Empathy for the handicapped										

18. Sense of humor												
19. Honoring grandparents, relatives												
20. Fixing things with tools												
21. Cooperation												
22. Personal philosophy of life												
23. Expressing feelings												
24. Risking sharing ideas												
25. Sexual attitudes												
26. Government, politics												
27. God, Deity												
28. Temper, anger, self-control												
29. Resolving disagreements												
30. Conscientiousness												
31. Taking care of property												
32. Death, suffering												
33. Compassionate service												
34. Domestic skills												
35. Punctuality												
36. Sabbath day observance												
37. Temple preparation												
38. Tithing												

true happiness does not come from material things, but from understanding the gospel, serving others, and the joy that comes from one's own labor? Perhaps more neighborly acts of service to widows, divorcees, and others in need would help involve your children in unselfish acts of charity.

(7) *Reading good books.* Fathers are very important in setting an example of reading. Children should be encouraged to read books and good literature. One way of doing this is to consistently read to them when they are little; when they are old enough to read they should read back to you. As they enter school, you can provide some incentives for them by evaluating each book they bring to you to inspect and you can pay them an amount of money—twenty-five or fifty cents or so for each book—depending on its quality. They can earn money by reading and you will find that their educational marks will improve. Most of our educational process is dependent on our reading ability. By the time they are teens, hopefully, they will be "hooked" on the value of good reading materials and your subsidy can end. There is too much time spent before the television and not enough time in good literature and current events.

(9) *Manners.* How polite are your children? at the table? answering the telephone? the front door? What do they do when you introduce them to a stranger or a member of the ward? There is much that can be taught children as to appropriate deportment and manners. Practice with them answering the phone and the front door. Teach them good table manners, both by instruction and modeling.

(11) *Money management practices.* What are you doing to help your children learn to budget, to save for things they want in the future? Suppose you review with them the elements of your budget, your expenses, so that they see both the necessity of having a job that pays well and the need to budget family resources wisely. You might want to give them a slip of paper and have them guess the monthly costs for various expenses you typically have

(rent, food, car payments, etc.). Then go back and give from your checkbook the actual costs you incur for these items, so that they gain some perspective on the essential expenses in managing a home.

(13) *Sportsmanship.* Sometimes even our Church athletic programs are so competitive that we fail to live gospel principles on the court and field. What are you doing to teach your children to win and lose gracefully? What are your children learning about other people who have greater skills than they have? Do they see them as evil, sneaky, cheating? There is much we can do in our family home evening activities to teach our children to win and lose without being poor sports and to improve their skills by sacrifice and hard work.

(17) *Empathy for the handicapped.* Children are sometimes rude to other children with handicaps. What are you doing to teach your children to be kind, empathic, and sensitive to those who are temporarily or permanently in need of some assistance with wheelchairs, opening doors, and companionship? We invited a blind girl over to our family home evening and had her share with the children the challenges of being unable to see. Then we went down the street a short distance, blindfolded the children, and had them try to walk back to our home with the aid of her white cane. They learned a little more about empathy and understanding of others who may not have the same physical blessings as they have.

(18) *Sense of humor.* There are plenty of challenges in life that test our sense of humor. Taking a week or two to collect jokes and cartoons and then sharing them in a family home evening will help develop a smile and an appreciation for humorous events in our lives.

(20) *Fixing things.* Many times fathers complain that their children won't stick around and help them finish a job. Fathers are often impatient, however, with their little children's mistakes with wrenches, pliers, and screwdrivers. Remember, Dad, that you were once a kid and required patience as you learned to use tools. If you are

kind and patient with your children when they help you, you will find that they do enjoy working side by side with you. Otherwise, they will slip away to do more rewarding things. Help your children learn repair and maintenance skills around the house so that they can fix broken items. You will save expensive labor costs (hopefully) by not having to call professionals on routine and minor repairs.

(25) *Sexual attitudes.* We need to realize that it is our parental responsibility to teach sacred principles of sex and procreation at home, and we need to come to grips with doing it. By the time most parents think their children are old enough for sex education, they are a year or two too late. However, even then, it is important for your children to know that *you know!* (Do you remember, when you were a kid, thinking, "If my folks knew what I know?") Sex education is not something that you do once and it is over. You need to have a number of sessions over the years as your children mature and can understand your cautions and the blessings that come from chastity. In fact, when they are teenagers you may need a consistent approach to sexual attitudes concerning infatuation, love, the importance of remaining worthy of a temple marriage, the place of intimacy in dating and marriage, physiology—menstruation, pregnancy, childbirth, "wet-dreams"—and gospel perspective on bearing and rearing children. It matters that you take the responsibility to see that your children are clear about responsible sexuality—particularly in a world that has lost its direction on this issue. (You may want to obtain a copy of the Church booklet entitled *A Parent's Guide* from your local distribution center. It contains some helpful advice on this subject.)

(36) *Sabbath day observance.* What are you teaching your children about the wise use of the Sabbath? Are they sleeping in longer because with the "block program" they don't have to get up for early meetings? What about fasting? prayer? gospel study? Is your home a home of Sabbath observance? There are many good dramatized tapes and Church publications for the little ones. The *New*

Era and the *Ensign* are outstanding sources of good Sabbath family reading as a complement to the scriptures.

(37) *Temple preparation.* Before your children go on a mission or marry in the temple, perhaps you could read and study together the Pearl of Great Price, especially Moses 2–5. You might even discuss with them some of the questions asked of those seeking a temple recommend, so that you can prepare your children as to what the bishop and stake president will ask them—and help them make that preparation. The questions represent a minimum level of worthiness, and our children should understand why they are meaningful issues in the life of a worthy Latter-day Saint.

By taking the time to teach your children the gospel and other principles of a happy, fulfilling life, you will help them to appreciate the breadth of the gospel plan. Best wishes, Dad, as you teach the fine spirits the Lord has given you to rear, and may you bless this earth with quality children who will contribute to the progress of righteousness in the most important dispensation of the gospel yet given to man.

Toward a   11
Zion Family

I remember growing up with the feeling that every other talk I heard in Church and every other lesson I was taught at Mutual was about the Word of Wisdom. A couple of friends and I used to keep track during general conference of how often the topic came up. It just seemed like the worst kind of overkill to us. Now, seeing the unrelenting tidal wave of drug and alcohol abuse sweep through our society, it is clear that the Lord was forewarning us.

Perhaps it's because I have such tender hopes for the strength and purity of my own children and because I desire so intensely for them to have the kind of rich and rewarding family life that Geri and I experience that I am sensitive to the amount of counsel we receive from Church leaders about family relations. Conference speakers repeatedly stress family themes. Articles on every aspect of marriage and parenting have appeared regularly in the *Ensign*. Obviously, the same kind of forewarning is occurring.

As a matter of professional interest, I do a great deal of reading about techniques of family relations, different types of therapy, and results of research done on marriages and families. Over and over I am struck with the inescapable conclusion that any technique, no matter how successful, becomes a gimmick if it is not energized and charged with a theological perspective of the family in eternity. If I do not keep that vision clearly before me I find myself faltering in my commitment to be a strong, stable marriage partner and a loving, positive role model for my children. Our theology has the most powerful motivation for parents that could possibly exist. Refusing to refresh my vision of it is like pulling the cord from the outlet but continuing to push the vacuum cleaner and wondering why the carpet doesn't get clean.

I see that the responsibility clearly begins with me—as it does with every individual. When I am prepared to function as a high-quality marriage partner, then Geri and I do extremely well. From that basic foundation, we can bring up our children so that they understand the purpose of their mortal probation and help carry out the Lord's work.

Key principles that I keep returning to—my personal ten commandments to keep me on the right path for my family—may be helpful to you as well.

1. *Make the plan of salvation an overall guide for righteous living.* If I find that my family relations are out of whack, chances are that my eternal perspective has slipped, that I've forgotten my heavenly parents and the atonement of our Savior and am feeling impatient or angry because selfish interests are intruding. I remember feeling called sharply to account one time by reading 1 John 4:20: "If a man say, I love God, and hateth his brother [children, in my case], he is a liar; for he that loveth not his brother whom he hath seen [or lived with], how can he love God whom he hath not seen?"

2. *Build strength into your marriage.* Geri and I take great comfort in our eternal sealing, but we know it's not going

to work unless we do. The separations and divorces of fine Latter-day Saint couples we know are a sobering reminder to us that no marriage is immune from problems and that our test is handling those problems successfully.

If I feel any kind of strain or distance in my relationship with Geri, I ask myself questions like these: How much time are we giving each other? Do we talk kindly with each other about our marriage and family? Do I have some negative habits that are choking our happiness? Do I communicate how much I value her love and her contribution to the family? Do I feel that my own contribution is valued?

I recall once talking with a recently married couple about some problems they were experiencing in dividing up the household chores. It didn't seem to be merely a matter of who had the most time, energy, or interest in seeing that a particular task got done; it had to do with some fixed ideas as to who should do them. I was puzzled until I heard Hal say, rather emphatically, "But this is the way we always did it."

"We?" I asked.

"Sure," he said. "My family."

"So when you say 'we' you don't mean you and Judy?" I probed gently. "And when you say 'my family' you aren't talking about you two?"

He was a bright young man. I have never seen such a series of revelations run so quickly across a face. Sometimes we do things out of habit from the family we grew up in. We assumed that since that is the way "we" did it, it must be the best way. Every couple has adjustments to make, and no one comes from the one true family. Marriage is a profound commitment to teach and learn from each other. Learning to be therapeutic with each other is a great task in marriage. When I cultivate an attitude of learning, loving, blessing, and honoring Geri, I find that I can hardly wait to be with her, to find out what she's been doing, to hear her ideas, and to hear her response to mine. It's an adventure in partnership.

3. *Be sensitive to the atmosphere you contribute to your home.* Here are some questions I ask myself every now and then on my way home from work: Are my children glad to see me when I come home or do they quietly disappear when I drive in the driveway or come in the house? Do they like our home? Do they want their friends to meet us? Are they proud of us? Am I really interested in their friends and their activities?

I learned a great lesson in home atmosphere from watching my wife approach our preschoolers, sitting on the floor absorbed in something. "Hi, honey," she would greet one of them, "can I help you with anything?" After years of this greeting, it's no wonder that they now come in and seek her out for a kiss, and ask her, "Can I help you with anything?"

Many times, of course, it's simply, "Look at this!" or "Got any cookies?" but this attitude of accessibility and a clear willingness to be of service communicates something precious about my wife's contribution to our home.

4. *Invest the time to understand and strengthen each child.* Sometimes a father will say to me, "But what do you *do* with a baby? He can't even talk yet." Oddly enough, I find the same father expressing helplessness in the relationship as the child gets older: "But what do you *do* with a four-year-old? Can't read. Can't even sit through a baseball game." And then wondering why he still has nothing to say to his sixteen-year-old son.

What do you do with a baby? You hug him, talk to him, sing nonsense rhymes in his ear, feed him mashed bananas and wipe up the mess afterwards, change his diaper, and rock him when he cries. What do you do with a four-year-old? Just watch the four-year-old for a few minutes, see what he's playing with, and then gently get down on his level and ask, "Would you like me to play too?"

Sometimes when children are in their teens, we withdraw because we feel uncertain about their new size, their maturity, their own awkwardness and ineptness in social situations. But that's the very time when your companionship, encouragement, and love are most needed.

If there's one thing we've learned about social problems through the decades of the Great Society and the War on Poverty it's that problems don't go away by turning our heads or by throwing money at them. Children aren't problems, but they can cause problems and they can certainly have problems. Do you know your children well enough to sense when a problem is coming up? Have you struggled with the Lord, fasting for direct inspiration about what a particular child needs?

> "Fathers, if you wish your children to be taught in the principles of the gospel, . . . if you wish them to be obedient to and united with you, love them! and prove to them that you do love them by your every word or act to them. For your own sake, for the love that should exist between you and your boys—however wayward they might be, . . . when you speak or talk to them, do it not in anger; do it not harshly, in a condemning spirit. Speak to them kindly; get down and weep with them, if necessary, and get them to shed tears with you if possible. Soften their hearts; get them to feel tenderly towards you. Use no lash and no violence, but . . . approach them with reason, with persuasion and love unfeigned. With this means, if you cannot gain your boys and your girls, . . . there will be no means left in the world by which you can win them to yourselves." (President Joseph F. Smith, *Liahona, The Elders' Journal*, 17 Oct. 1911, pp. 260–61; quoted in Ezra Taft Benson, "Great Things Required of Their Fathers," *Ensign*, May 1981, p. 34.)

5. *Build emotional and spiritual dimensions into your family life.* No matter how beautifully you do the dishes, they're going to get dirty again. No matter how closely you shave, the whiskers will be back tomorrow. No matter how well you listened on Tuesday, you're going to need to spend high-quality time on Thursday. Your children are probably not going to think first of prayer when they've got a problem unless they've seen you, hundreds of times, implore the Lord for blessings and assistance.

Emotional closeness and spirituality aren't cosmic, technicolor productions. They're simply and consistently doing over and over and over, day after day, week after week, the kinds of activities that invite the Spirit of the Lord into your home. They are simple, specific prayers. They are family home evenings with a lot of laughter mixed with serious gospel topics. They're consistent worship together at church. They're a love of the scriptures and regular study of them.

Beware of two traps in your effort to build spirituality. Some people equate behavior with feelings and spend inordinate amounts of time forcing certain types of behavior. Reverence, for example, is not the same thing as simply being quiet. Being able to rattle off memorized scriptures is not the same thing as feeling the Lord as a living presence for your teenager. Identify your own feelings with your children: what makes you feel reverent and what you feel like doing when you're reverent, or what loving feels like and how loving people act.

The second trap is false piety. As Mormons, we have a strong culture. We have our own codes of modesty and diet, our right answers for almost any question; a clearly specified list of where we should be and when; a checklist of what makes us acceptable, worthy, and righteous. The problem is that some people, in a sincere but misguided effort to become righteous, mistake the checklist for the gospel. We can easily become hypocrites, scrupulously paying tithing but being unkind to others who don't quite fit in. We can also become self-righteous and tell ourselves that we are sacrificial martyrs in a noble cause that no one else recognizes.

I tend to mistrust people whose manner suggests they are living the gospel in every detail but who aren't also having a great time. My definition of a successful Latter-day Saint is a happy one. Help your children tell the false from the true in emotional warmth and in spirituality.

6. *Genuinely express pride and praise to both your spouse and your children frequently.* For some reason, most of us are fairly stingy in commending things well done. I've very

seldom seen a situation where negative criticism—unless followed immediately by increased love—didn't actually make things worse. A lazy child gets sulky as well as lazy. An awkward one drops more things. A grouchy one gets angrier.

In contrast, a little hug, a tender whisper, a happy delight in the other person creates a kind of sunshine in the atmosphere that we'd be crazy to pass up for more gloom. Mark Twain once said, "I can live for two months on a good compliment" (Donald O. Bolander, comp., *Instant Quotation Dictionary* [Little Falls, New Jersey: Career Institute, 1969], p. 206).

Joseph Smith said that it is important to one's faith to know "that the course of life which he pursues is according to the will of God." That knowledge, he continues, "is essentially necessary to enable him to have that confidence in God without which no person can obtain eternal life." (*Lectures on Faith*, 6:2.)

I think we all know from our experiences with the Holy Ghost in this life what Joseph Smith is saying. When we are able to serve someone, that accompanying glow is, I believe, a faint taste of the Father's joy in our willingness to love and serve each other. When we carry out an assignment in the Church, we have a spiritual confirmation that our work is acceptable. In our families, it's important to celebrate the good things that happen. I try to recognize those little flickers of pride and happiness when Geri or one of the children do something to please me, and I tell them so. It makes the love grow in our family.

7. *Seek feedback from your family about how things are working.* It is a truism that you've never been married before this life and that these are the first children you've ever had. It is also a truism that our heavenly parents want us to learn eternally true principles from this collection of unique individuals. Often people will ask me what the best book is on marriage or family relations, and my reaction always is, "They have never written a book on your spouse, or your children yet. Your family is your best

source of help, and provides the best data you can receive.'' The record you jointly make will be recorded in heaven.

Seek the views of your spouse and children on all aspects of your family living. Sometimes a group discussion is the best way. Sometimes a one-on-one visit is more effective.

Accept suggestions from your children when you can, and if possible honor their requests to do some things differently. When you can't, explain clearly and courteously. Your children need to know that you consider their feelings and that their suggestions are worthy ones. If you can make them a sounding board for ideas that affect their lives, you might be pleasantly surprised at how easily they turn to you with the same process during their teen years when they need to develop trust in their own ability to make intelligent choices.

Remember not to make any decisions for them that they can make for themselves, but always be ready to review correct principles and walk through possible consequences with them.

8. *Teach your children what you want them to know and be.* Geri and I are painfully aware that the world will teach our children in every area where we don't take that responsibility. Becky came home from junior high school with the declaration that she thought two or three children were sufficient for any family to have in today's world. Somehow we realized that we had never discussed the perspective of family size, a subject that we both have some thoughts about.

Lots of teaching occurs informally, but an early tradition of gathering together to discuss specific topics is valuable. We've found that our preschoolers don't need reasons for rules, but they do need the rules. We make a habit of explaining the reason at the same time as the rule, so that when they're ready to challenge the rule a little later the reason for it already has a head start in their minds.

Another teaching point is prevention. Before Terri entered junior high, I had a special father's interview with her before her blessing. I told her she would probably hear obscenities, encounter graffiti inconsistent with our standards, and be invited to participate in behavior that might seem adventuresome and appealing. I asked her specific questions to review her knowledge about some of our family values, her personal attitudes, and some doctrinal points. I assured her of our love, of our desire that she have a wonderful, freeing experience in this new step in her education, and tried to be specific about the kind of power that wisdom would give her. Geri and I wanted her to be anxious *to meet* these new experiences, not anxious *about* them. When the scenario we had traced occurred pretty much as I had predicted, she was delighted to bring home reports of what had happened and how she had responded. Because we were able to praise her for making wise decisions instead of having to help her overcome the results of bad decisions, we feel that she had a wonderful year.

I encourage parents to make a list of topics they want to share with their children. This list can be as far-reaching as the plan of salvation and as grimly practical as taking precautions against sexual abuse. (Many of the topics we use were given in the previous chapter.) See what kinds of aids are available from the ward library, your nearest Church distribution center, and Church publications, as well as community resources.

9. *Make time for family matters.* If this is starting to sound like the other nine commandments in some form or other, it's because it's true. The price of effective parenting is your time. There is no substitute for it, and neglecting to pay this price when the bill comes up only means that we will have to pay it with interest later. Part of the price is reading stories, working together, saying "I love you," attending school functions, and visiting with their teachers to keep current on academic and spiritual progress all take time. Pay the price to know.

Behavior problems are typically relationship problems. If a child seems to be out of harmony with you or with the family as a whole, check their relationships. Is this one child mirroring strain between you and your spouse? Is it between you and the child? Are their brothers and sisters involved? Is the peer group creating tension? How about the child's teachers? A simple guideline is: correct the relationship and behavioral problems will subside.

10. *Teach your children to reach beyond the family hearth to serve others.* Children have to be given enormous quantities of love before they can give love to others—both as a matter of personal security and also as a matter of modeling. Sometimes they are uncertain about how to translate family rules for sharing, kindness, and honesty outside the family circle where a different set of rules seem to apply. Involve them in service so they can see, from your own modeling, what to do and how to do it. How can our children learn to love missionary work if we fail to set the example? Working with nonmembers or inactive families, or visiting the elderly and lonely, can bring good feelings for even the little children. Discuss ways to bring individuals and families into your home for friendshipping.

Quoting Richard Eyre, Elder L. Tom Perry has given us a great perspective on this matter.

> What we must remember is that the Church exists within the world and has the purpose of saving and preparing the world. If we who are within the Church associate only with each other [or just the actives], give our time and our means only to internal Church causes, we remove ourselves from the world. Then two particularly negative results occur: first, we become more parochial, more narrow, less compassionate. We lose our perspective and have fewer chances to use and to spread the real gospel. Second, the people around us and the causes around us lose the potential benefit of our association and our help. The world becomes for them, and for us, a less happy place to live. The fact is that our tendency is to dwell on the things that make us different from the world. Our basic belief is in Christ. The traditional values

we embrace, our hopes, our dreams, our freedom and liberty are all shared by right-minded, principled Christian people throughout the world. If we build bridges rather than walls, we begin to see that the gospel principles always unite and never separate. ("In the World," *Brigham Young University 1981 Fireside and Devotional Speeches* [Provo: University Publications, BYU, 1981], pp. 5–6.)

In conclusion, each family striving to build Zion will have its own unique constellation of values and attitudes, its own emphases and talents. Each successful family will be dedicated to developing happy, healthy individuals who have the discipline to work hard at goals and to establish relationships of their own built on love and respect. And we're not in this venture alone. Who could want our success more than our Heavenly Father? And who has more power to bring about success from our sometimes inept though well-meaning efforts?

Jesus pointed out, "Where your treasure is, there will your heart be also" (Matthew 6:21). For me, for you—let's make that treasure place our home and family.

Index

Church activity, 54
Church attendance, 154, 158
Church, complement to home, 13
Church News, 2
Commitment, 6
Communication, family, 155
  improvement of, 122–24
  in marriage, 42–47
  levels of, 110–13
  skills, 32–33
  through intimacy, 139–46
  with children, 80, 153–55, 165–70,
    183–84
  with spouse, 80–81
Companionship, 42–47, 122
Compassion, 22
Contention, 120
Cooperation, 102
Counseling, marriage, 3–7
Counselors, 146
  marriage, 3, 7, 33, 115, 141, 144–45
Couples (book), 37
Courtship, 4, 13, 19, 97–99, 100
  See also Dating
Courtesy, 33
Covenants, 5, 8, 22
Cowdery, Oliver, 150
Criticism, 6

— D —

Dating, 4, 12, 13, 19, 32
  at age sixteen, 67–68
  inadequate for marriage prepara-
    tion, 39, 94–95, 103
  time important in, 97
Death, 11–12, 172–73
Debt, 89–90
  See also Money management
"Deepening Our Love Commitment" (list), 126–31
Defensiveness, 4, 6
Degrees of glory, 48, 66
  See also Plan of salvation
Discipline, 148, 154, 164–65
  See also Children
Divorce, 30, 32, 40, 94, 182
  due to selfishness, 26
  hardship brought by, 4
  not a growth option, 53
  sometimes justifiable, 7–8, 54
  statistics, 2
  through transgression, 8

Divorced persons, 54–55
Doctrine and Covenants, 29
Doctrines of Salvation (book), 63
Drug abuse, 180
Durham, G. Homer, arr., *Evidences
  and Reconciliations,* 28–29

— E —

Education, 173
Elias, priesthood keys restored by,
  64–66
Elijah, priesthood keys restored by,
  64, 66–67
Emotional bonding, 109–31
Emotional stability, 51–52
Emotional strength, 184–85
Empathy, 177
Eternal families, 11–35, 181
Evidences and Reconciliations (book),
  28–29
Evil, 27
Exaltation, 21, 23–27, 48, 62–63, 66,
  134
Eyre, Richard, on service, 189–90

— F —

Faith, 40
Families, 7
  bonds, 11
  common problems of, 75–91
  eternal nature of, 11–35, 181
  importance of, 11
  little kingdoms, 62–63
  ordained by God, 1
  relationships in, 30–33, 41–42,
    147–79
  traditions of, 155–59
  unity in, 91
  See also Home
Family councils, 29, 153, 157, 165
Family home evening, 29, 104, 155,
  165, 167, 177, 185
  counsel of prophets on, 71, 149
  purpose of, 153
  a tradition, 157
Family prayer, 29, 71, 124, 158, 165,
  166
Family reunions, 157–58
Fasting, 120, 178, 184
Fathers, 42, 89, 152–53, 162–79
  calling of, 61–63
  See also Parenting